FROM A TEACHER TO PARENTS

STORIES

TO

HEAL YOUR LIFE

SO YOU CAN

HELP YOUR CHILD SUCCEED

ANDRENE BONNER

New York

From A Teacher To Parents

Stories To Heal Your Life So You Can Help Your Child Succeed

Copyright© 2017 Andrene Bonner

All Rights Reserved. Scanning, uploading, electronic storage or sharing of any part of this book is strictly prohibited under the US Copyright Act of 1976. Except in brief quotations, permission is required from the author or publisher: contact@sisalpublishing.com.

www.sisalpublishing.com

Published by: Sisal Publishing

Library of Congress Cataloging in Publication Data

Book Developer: Faith Nelson, Story Depot

Cover Design by Les Solot

ISBN-13: 978-0-9975905-2-4 (Paperback)

ISBN-10: 0-9975905-2-1

Bonner, Andrene, 1955-

Author's Photograph by Yvonne Taylor [From Author's Personal Archives]

Printed in the United States of America
First Edition

Publisher's Disclaimer

From A Teacher To Parents: Stories To Heal Your Life So You Can Help Your Child Succeed is a work of non-fiction. The author has drawn on her personal life experiences and other events to recreate real and true to life stories. Names, locations and occupations have been changed to protect privacy.

Dedication

Dedicated to the memory of my parents

Gwendoline Louise Anderson-Bonner

&

Egbert Bonner

Exceptional teachers who taught generations the value of an education.

For My Daughter...

Keisha Lloyd who constantly seeks out self-help tools to successfully raise her 21st century daughter, Jamaya.

Contents

Dedication i

For My Daughter… ii

Introduction v

Teachers and Mentors 1

Special Needs 10

Creativity 18

Mindfulness 24

Never Too Old To Learn 30

Courage 35

Love Practice 40

Sleep 46

Vocabulary For Life 50

Secrets Can Harm 56

Emotional Blackmail 62

Failure 67

Grief 72

Guiding Teens 77

Gratitude 83

Intention 87

People Pleasing 93

Forgiveness 98

Love Letters 105

Quantum Action 111

Nature's Season 117

Critical Thinking 122

Absence 127

Bust on the Bully 137

Ask Questions 144

Empathy 151

Confidence 157

Self-Control 164

Goal Setting 170

Sacred Space 175

Integrity 180

Effort 184

Adaptability 190

References 195

Acknowledgements 207

Literacy Gateway Institute 209

Introduction

When American poet Maya Angelou was eight years old, she was sexually abused by her mother's boyfriend. In confidence, she told her brother who then told the family and the family reported him to the authorities. The man went to jail but got out after only one day. Four days later Maya's uncles allegedly meted out their own brand of justice and the man was found dead. Maya, believing herself to have caused his death, lost her urge to speak and remained that way for five years. Imagine the trauma of rape, the young girl's fear of the brutality and the misplaced guilt for his death. Add to that, the reality of 1930s America in the middle of the Great Depression, when life was even more difficult for African Americans. Today, it would be easy to get psychological counseling. Back then, creativity and ingenuity would have been the psychologist's couch.

In *I Know Why The Caged Bird Sings*, Maya Angelou, then called Marguerite, details a moving account of the event leading up to her being freed from her five year silence. On the day in question, the teacher, Mrs. Flowers, shopped at Maya's grandmother's store. When it was suggested that Maya's brother Bailey should carry Mrs. Flower's shopping bag, the offer was turned down.

"Thank you Mrs. Henderson. I'd prefer Marguerite, though." My name was beautiful when she said it.

"I've been meaning to talk to her, anyway." They gave each other age-group looks." What ensues is teatime with Mrs. Flowers and Maya's earthshaking eye-opening introduction to *A Tale Of Two Cities*. The teacher's clever lecture on the value of poetry and the human voice hit home. Marguerite breaks her five years of silence with the words, "Yes Ma'am" and the rest is history. She has written many works of fiction and nonfiction, given inspirational talks to millions and penned poems for two presidential inaugurations.

What did Maya mean when she wrote, "They gave each other age-group looks?" Grandma Henderson realized that Maya loved reading but needed creative therapy. African American teachers were well-read and deservingly held in high regard then. Mrs. Flowers was the solution. Knowing how close-knit communities were during that time, both women would have had several conversations about the troubled child. Teacher and parent or caregiver must have planned Operation Rescue Marguerite with strong intention and ingenuity.

How brilliant to use English Literature, which the child loved, to begin to heal the emotional wounds. Maya, writing years later about the moment says:

> "I didn't question why Mrs. Flowers had singled me out for attention, nor did it occur to me that Momma might have asked her to give me a little talking-to. All I cared about was that she had made tea cookies for me and read to me from her favorite book."

The event was a collaboration, a coming together of persons with a common goal. Maya had the emotional raw material, latent strength and resilience within herself. They just needed to be freed. As caregiver, protector and grandmother, Mrs. Henderson was creating a healing environment at home to support the children, even Maya's reading habit. She knew when to get outside help. Mrs. Flowers was the fully invested teacher and healer. I believe neither of the women, on their own, could have been the sole catalyst for Maya's healing. They are co-heroines in her personal drama.

Whether it is the 21st Century classroom or a 1930s living room in Stamps Arkansas, teachers and parents putting their heads together, move mountains. As a school teacher and seminar facilitator I am hopeful that all my students will do well. In fact, I am mandated, by law, to follow certain guidelines in preparing my high school students for a bright future. However, a tidy academic life filled with aced tests, certificates, graduation and scholarships is a myth for some students. School life is an epic struggle and for the frustrated group being left behind, the reason sometimes has little to do with IQ. I needed to make a difference with this group in my classroom and I knew that in order to change behavior, I needed teacher-parent relationships like that between Mrs. Henderson and Mrs. Flowers.

In today's schools, there are more parents like Mrs. Henderson than we realize. They are courageous strategists. They are aware of the emotional minefield in which we live. They know students can't cordon off and lock away emotional problems, hoping they don't rear their ugly heads in the classroom. Life isn't like that. Students suffer from stress, inertia, lack of focus, raging hormones, awkwardness, you name it, the stumbling blocks are there. Parents of underperforming students are tired of standing on the sidelines in this quest for excellence. They want to break the cycle of the past. During my various seminar experiences, I have been approached by parents who say, "I need help." They are overwhelmed by the complexity of life. They ask, "What do I need to do?"

In one of my seminars, a mom I'll call Mrs. Brown needed to help her child prepare for pre-college exams. The student was scoring in the lowest percentile –failing every test and turning in poorly done homework. Mom confessed that she was unable to truly monitor her daughter's progress at home. Disciplining was a shouting match instead of a strategy session. I sensed there was more she was not saying but one thing I was sure about, parent-teachers meetings were not going to be enough. I started with what I knew. Mom's lack of subject matter knowledge, I could deal with. In fact, that was what my seminars were about – helping the parent learn what the student was learning. In a subsequent workshop session, I learnt that Mrs. Brown hadn't finished high school and I was able to tailor the lessons accordingly.

As the work sessions progressed, the surprise gift was that Mrs. Brown became more tuned into her feelings of inadequacy. Though I am not a psychologist, I discovered that she was struggling with unresolved issues from the past. Her parents didn't send her to school after the age of fifteen. She stayed home and worked the small farm. I gave her whatever information and encouragement I could. Before, she had been fighting an invisible enemy, but could now courageously stare down this villain. Now she had a chance at winning.

Contrary to what a child will tell you about the teacher he or she admires most, parents are the most influential teachers in the world. Now don't get me wrong. I love teaching. I feel the rush of pride as my successful students walk to the podium on graduation day and collect their well-earned diploma and extra prizes. They keep up with me after graduation and I feel even more proud of their progress. But guess what! Whatever the parental relationship is on the spectrum – nurturing to dysfunctional–Mom and Dad have a profound impact. I am a subject matter expert in the school environment. I take care of the children from 8 a.m. – 4 p.m., but I take care of them knowing that it is a partnership effort. Mrs. Brown was one such partner who was going through the self-healing process. Though her daughter was already a teen, she did not believe it was too late to change her attitude and change her life in order to help her child.

This book, *Stories to Heal Your Life*, offers parents a way to get personal with their own emotional roadmap. Where have they come from? What have they learnt from their parents? What has influenced them along the way? What have they inadvertently passed on to their children? By no means am I saying parents are the root cause of all of a student's problems. Parents are the first and most influential teachers. No matter the school age of the child, once parents are aware of the depth of the role they can play in helping to change behavior, they can correct their course and help their children develop more problem solving skills, courage, adaptability, self-discipline, self-care, even vocabulary, among other strengths. We want students to become successful, well-adjusted happy adults but school/early education can be a minefield.

The relationship between the parent, the teacher, and the student needs to be one of harmony. In today's competitive, stressful climate we need to up the ante. We need to be more strategic in our self-work. Our children, our students need more than a survival toolkit for the future. They need an emotional toolkit to give them resilience and help them thrive and shape their world. Parents, who are themselves emotionally well, can help spark these attributes.

This book is not for parents who are self-aware and have well-adjusted, high performers. This book is for the exhausted and overwhelmed parent of the underperformer who wants to help engineer the best future for his or her child and is willing to make a change in order to do it. The stories and examples in this book help parents identify the harmful recurring patterns and habits that we hold dear, that we also inadvertently pass on to our children. The stories are a wake-up call to grow our awareness in order to break the tyranny of fear, illiteracy, abuse, abandonment and toxic relationships.

The stories can be read all at once or in bite-sized pieces, once a day. The affirmations can be taped to your mirror or your refrigerator and inserted as reminders in your cell-phones. They can start your day or be read before bedtime along with other uplifting literature you may have. If we are operating in a constant state of mindfulness that our life as a parent is always evolving in front of our children, who mimic our every action or inaction, then we are poised to experience more success, harmony and love. In turn, this helps to nurture the joyful curiosity and develop the emotional strength children need to succeed in their academic and social environment.

Chapter 1

Teachers and Mentors

None of us got where we are solely by pulling ourselves up by our bootstraps. We got here because somebody – a parent, a teacher, an Ivy League crony or a few nuns – bent down and helped us pick up our boots.

–Thurgood Marshall

Some call it Spiderman's Spidey Senses, intuition, gut feelings, second sight. Whatever you call it, when it comes to raising children we need it in spades. Unfortunately, stress undermines our ability to tune into this magical state when we need it most. These little people we raise constantly push the boundaries. When that happens, we need eyes in the back of our heads to raise our children well. Better yet, we need helpers on our sometimes challenging journey.

"She is not doing it, Ms. Bonner, over my dead body!"

My heart skipped and skidded. I was on the phone with my daughter's French teacher Monsieur Durand. What had my daughter not done? In that short amount of time, I ran several horrible scenarios in my mind.

"What's the matter Monsieur Durand?" I stuttered.

"Your daughter is going to do French II. She is one of the best, if not the best in class. But she has signed up for Health Science instead."

I heaved a sigh of relief. The situation was not as bad as I thought. The matter could be fixed, whatever the cause. This was the conversation I wanted to have with any teacher. Some people may think it heavy handed but I love a teacher who is all in. My daughter, who was excellent at French, had decided to do another subject. She loved French. What had precipitated this sudden change? I found out that she had decided to follow her group of friends to the new class. That was her sole reason for skipping French! She needed to be with her friends.

Needing to be reasonable, I discussed the matter when she came home. I cajoled and got nowhere. So I gave her an ultimatum. She could eat with her friends during break and chat during lunch but I put my foot down. She was not going to run away from French II because she loved her friends. That was not a good enough reason. Needless to say, that semester, she took French II. It was important for me to know whether or not peer pressure played a role. But it was even more vital to partner with an emotionally invested teacher.

In the hometown of my childhood, we used to have old women sitting on the verandahs watching us as we walked by after school. If we forgot their presence and did anything rude, we would hear a chorus of warnings, questions, even our names blast out from the verandahs. Heads full of grey hair would pop up over the rails. *I'm going to tell your mother what you're doing!* We need extra pairs of eyes to avert disaster that might be waiting in the wings.

My mother was a strong mentor to the next generation in our family. Fortunately, the passage of time had lightened her heavy hand. She didn't have to physically discipline her grandchildren and great grandchildren. When we were growing up and misbehaved, we would be sent to retrieve her instrument of discipline. At the least, we would get strong taps on the butt with it. She needed to get her message across and that was the way at the time. The young ones, however, got an objective voice, gently imparting wisdom.

Since Mother had been a teacher, the young ones were learning their ABCs at a very early age. Sprinkled between the ABCs and the counting exercises were admonitions and guidance. Stories had little messages wrapped in them that taught the children about good behavior, creativity and the like. My daughter adored her Grandma and respected her opinions. She absorbed the lessons.

For the most part my daughter was well-behaved at home. By age fourteen, however, she turned into a different person. Neither Grandma nor I could get through to her. It's as if the inner good girl had been plucked out and replaced with a disagreeable two-year old. "No I don't want to!" was a constant in every conversation.

"I want my Dad. You wouldn't understand Mom!"

Old school parent that I was, I never asked her what she wanted to do. She missed her father keenly and often told me so. Her offences were not egregious. They were little sins punctuated with sass about her missing Dad. At first, I was angry about these requests. I saw them as a sign that she was an ungrateful child. Who was the one who had changed her pampers! The more I threatened repercussions for her bad behavior, the more she pushed the boundaries. Things came to a head when one school evening she didn't come home on time. By nightfall there was no word from her. Worried to death, I called her friends with questions. Had she been kidnapped? I called my troops for help. Close to midnight, I got news that she was at the *World on Wheels* on Venice Boulevard, quite a ways from home. My cousin Nigel, a father figure who had been there for many of her important moments, took me to the rink to bring her home.

 After the incident, it was clear I needed to respond to her request to live with her dad. I was only too happy to do it but I rolled my eyes as I considered her luxury of choice. When I was growing up we didn't have those options. If you were unhappy with your parent, that was your lot. Her visit to Jamaica gave me time to contemplate on what I needed to learn about parenting. There were generational differences that I needed to address. I realized I needed to let go of some old-fashioned notions about raising kids.

 In hindsight, school was a touchy subject, a Pandora's Box I had to unpack. I was unaware of it at the time but I was still harboring some pain and resentment about my economic struggles during my high school years and thought my daughter had a 'free ride' in the US and was wasting it. In the US, failure of the 8th grade exam does not prevent you from going to a public high school. In Jamaica and other commonwealth countries, that failure, caused by test anxiety on exam day, meant economic punishment for your family. Your parents would pay for you to attend a public high school for the next five years and you had to buy your own textbooks.

I came from a family of five siblings and although my parents were educated civil servants living in an urban setting, they struggled to make ends meet. Compounded with the lack of a full scholarship, lower income meant not attending the school of my choice, walking too many miles to the bus stop on school days and staying home when there was no money for lunch. On the days I stayed home from school, I hid from the neighbors, embarrassed of my situation. A-Grade high schools were a class indicator. Not being afforded the opportunity to attend one of them was a badge of shame. The family's identity was intrinsically linked to this belief system. Unbeknownst to me, my conversations with my daughter were loaded with angst from this past. Those emotions made me reflect on the rich life I lived at this great high school where I excelled in the visual and performing arts. I was blind to the fact that my daughter had a right to live a different life. I never let her forget that she was more fortunate than me to be attending the Hollywood Performing Arts High School. I never let her forget that I paid for school when she went for free.

My daughter's visit to Jamaica proved to be a major turning point for both of us. She spent two semesters living with her dad and a surprise stepmom in Jamaica and learnt valuable life lessons. That was our last crisis.

God only knows what would have happened had I waited longer before sending my daughter to Jamaica. The incident reminds me that Oprah had to be sent to her dad, Vernon Winfrey in Nashville to temper her troublesome years. It proved a turning point for Oprah as well. The time spent in Nashville was a character builder. "I needed structure and attention. I required a lot of attention," Winfrey said in an interview. "When I was living with my mother I was ... rebellious ... I used to pull all kinds of pranks, ran away from home. When I got to my father's house, I never told another lie." Sometimes circumstances are such that we can't go it alone. I looked for help and the village came to my aid.

UC Davis Professor, Emmy Werner, followed individuals from infancy to adulthood in a study on resilience and recovery. What she found was that a third of the 698 Kauai children, although exposed to high risk factors from birth, absent fathers, alcoholics, physical abuse among other problems, turned out to be very resilient. She listed three types of "protective factors" forming the bedrock for their success: personality factors, a dependable family member and help from the community. These "high risk survivors" as she called them had the personality to thrive almost from birth. The second protective factor was strong family support - "a close bond with one competent, emotionally stable person who was sensitive to their needs." In a supportive community, she identified elders, teachers and church leaders among those providing mentorship. Boys and girls seemed to require a slightly different strategy. Boys needed a strong guiding hand and needed to be encouraged to express their emotions, while girls needed "reliable support from a female caregiver" and needed to be encouraged to be independent.

My daughter, Winfrey and Angelou prove the truth in Werner's observations. Children need to develop the building blocks of resilience early on the life journey. Whatever my daughter's personality, as a parent I needed to be proactive about helping her prepare to meet crisis head-on. After some resistance, I could. But, then, we didn't have the same level of distractions we have now. As a result of the damaging emotional programming bombarding our children today, we need to clear as much debris as possible from our personal emotional landscape in order to help them. Let the healing begin. As my daughter says, "trust the process."

Affirmation: *I see and understand my children. I am patient with them as they discover who they truly are. My job is to teach them how to love and how to become independent and responsible human beings. I am thankful for the angel mentors and teachers who help me along the way.*

Chapter 2

Special Needs

Each of us is a unique strand in the intricate web of life and here to make a contribution.

—Deepak Chopra

No two persons are alike. We come with our natural abilities, distinct talents that we express in diverse ways. We learn differently despite the fact that our schools are in some ways a one-size-fits-all system. We absurdly hope that all our students develop at the same pace emotionally, academically and socially but it doesn't always happen. Children with special needs face intense learning and development challenges. However, they have the potential to be successful if only we give them the quality attention they deserve in order to achieve that success.

Max's second son, Michael was not showing the development children reached at certain milestones. At three, her dearly beloved child wasn't speaking. At age four he wasn't reading. Max was going for a Ph.D. in education, for God's sake. Why couldn't she solve this problem? Why couldn't she get him to speak? She had to get him properly diagnosed. False hope came when the school misdiagnosed him with ADHD and gave him Ritalin to treat the problem.

At first, Michael's illness or condition caused the family great distress. Her husband buried his head in the sand and grew angry. Relatives whispered and tried to hide their embarrassment. Being primary caregiver, she had no such luxury. Max began to wage an epic battle to identify the problem and change what she could.

Since Michael was not speaking, the school labeled him retarded, did an Individualized Education Plan (IEP) and recommended he be moved to a special institution. Meanwhile, she continued to teach him and to make discoveries at home. He was a genius at math. Several institutions later, she proved that her son belonged in an environment that would support his high functioning skills in science and mathematics. Before long, that school was challenging him with complex math problems which he solved with ease, demonstrating mastery of the subject.

When Max learned that her fourth child, Joseph, was also diagnosed with ADHD, she was heartbroken. Joseph and Michael were nine years apart but not much had changed. Again, Max could see that he had been misdiagnosed. She would have to launch the battle all over again. There were still no support groups in her area. She yearned for camaraderie with others in her position. The specter of self-blame and helplessness overshadowed the day to day. Some days she needed counseling. She still couldn't believe that God had given her more than one child with this condition. "Say this isn't so. Why would God do this to me again? One child was enough—but two children!"

It was the early 80s, long before popular research; long before *Rain Man*. Then a lucky break from Yale. She came across Dr. Lorna Wing's groundbreaking article and other materials on Asperger Syndrome. The condition had a name. The symptoms covered in the material reflected those she had seen in both her sons - Asperger Syndrome, which apparently had been inherited from their dad. She viewed it as a tremendous challenge but now she was sure of one thing. They were not learning disabled. As the children developed, it was as if a lamp had been switched on and Max was beginning to focus less on the "so-called" tragedy and more on the moment and matters of the heart. Each child approached life with personal ingenuity, creativity and joy and so would she.

Max could see that although they struggled in some areas, one showed an affinity for math and science. The other had a propensity for things artistic. Both needed more time with the Speech Pathologist and social interaction exercises. They responded to the world in their own unique way. She started journaling their milestones and setbacks and as she wrote, her attitude changed and her heart opened. She began to praise them more often, her walls at home becoming a mosaic of special childhood moments.

The battle continued. Max read books on the subject. Back then, Google did not exist so it meant trips to libraries. She reached out to the *Special Needs Advocacy Network*, to learn as much as she could. Intent on giving it her all, she made the difficult decision to give up her career and completely devote her time to their care. The children needed full time supervision and advocacy and that proved to be the turning point. The classroom was not off limits to Max and she began showing up every day to observe her child's academic and social interactions. She wanted to see if what the teachers were doing worked. Objections went away and teachers eventually partnered fully with her to give the children what they needed. Bent on enriching their lives, she enrolled Michael in after school sporting activities and the cub scouts. Since Joseph was much younger, he got to run around the playing field to his heart's delight.

Max's struggle has not been without sacrifice. As if this personal drama wasn't enough, her husband, embarrassed by her overt public fight for the boys' education, divorced her. She was homeless for a time. The courts awarded full custody of the kids to their dad. Fortunately, she'd done enough foundational work with the boys, so they didn't lose their momentum. She had taken them through the worst. Ironically, she did such a good job that by the time the children were adults, their Asperger did not get in the way of their functioning. Max lost the children but she says it was worth the fight. She would rather see their success. Her case is extreme. Not all families demand this level of sacrifice.

Nowadays, wanting to create a community of parents with children who have Asperger Syndrome and other symptoms on the Autism Spectrum, Max has taken a bold step to establish a self-help group. She went back to college and earned her Ph.D. She has started a ministry to support families who are struggling with young and even adult children with special needs. With the knowledge and experience she has accumulated over the years, her program is an excellent resource for caregivers in the community.

What can we learn from Max? Relentless advocacy. She did three things exceptionally well. She did the research. She learnt the language. She became the back-up teacher to her boys. These three steps are still required today even with the increased awareness. She warns that parents who find themselves in need might be reluctant to seek help. There is still a stigma attached to the diagnosis.

These days, it's easy to get evaluations and treatments done for children on the spectrum. The numbers are increasing and it's not all due to lack of diagnosis. But more could be done. The emphasis is on the word "spectrum." Do all children need to pack the shelves at department stores or wash dishes at restaurants? Nothing is wrong with those jobs but some kids on the spectrum can do jobs requiring higher mental acuity. It is public knowledge that there are people with Asperger Syndrome who inspire and contribute to our world at high levels of functioning and scholarship.

Max tells the story that while she was a professor at Princeton, she met Professor John Forbes Nash, Nobel Prize winner for Mathematics and Economics who was also a professor at Princeton. Though he didn't have Asperger Syndrome, she shared that he showed visible signs of the mental illness, yet that did not stop him from becoming a first class educator. His compelling story inspired the Academy Award winning film, *A Beautiful Mind*. She felt the irony. She had fought the great fight to get her children the attention they deserved and an opportunity to study at Ivy League universities. They are now lending their talents to Fortune 100 companies and mentoring others as well. As the saying goes: seven children, seven different minds.

Love and celebrate the differences in our children. Max's willingness to "see" the children and their magnificence and not just their condition was the turning point in their lives. She became an intrepid explorer. It is important to ferret out the facts about our children's health and well-being. No matter the level of our education, we have to do the research, we have to learn the language and become teachers in the home environment. Too many parents today still leave the work up to the therapists. Some parents even look at therapy as an inconvenience. Max lost her husband to pride and a divorce but she didn't lose her grip on her children. These unique personalities must contribute their exceptional brand of goodness to humanity.

Affirmation: *I am becoming more aware that we all have something wonderful to offer the world. I let go of any feeling of superiority to others and I accept the greatness in our uniqueness.*

Chapter 3

Creativity

If you hear a voice within you say 'you cannot paint,' then by all means paint, and that voice will be silenced.

−Vincent Van Gogh

"Mama, I love being an actress," I cried in agony as she snatched my bag with my costumes and script. "You better take this drama nonsense out of your head. You are not going anywhere this evening. God would not be seen in the theatre. It is the devil's playground." I was sixteen years old on my way to the dress rehearsal for the classic comedy, *The Bird on Nellie's Hat*. This was going to be my first commercial play. Three months earlier, I had received a coveted drama scholarship for my performance in the annual school's drama festival. I was on top of the world. Now, in a split second it was snatched away from me. I was bewildered, angry. A select private audience would be arriving at the theatre in three hours. How could I be a no-show after six weeks of rehearsals? I pleaded, "But mama, this is what I want to do. I am good at it!"

"Don't 'but mama' me!" she hissed.

She was hearing none of it. Mama could be unrelenting sometimes. I recognized the steel in her voice. Cold sweat rolled down my body. I trembled, battling fear and the urge to flip the sofa on its back. "Two bulls can't reign in one pen," she had often warned. The threat of retribution if I disobeyed was real. I rebelled and went, weeping all the way to rehearsal. After practice, I returned home to find all doors locked. My youngest sister rescued me. Rehearsals continued in secret but I was never fully focused on the task. I feared my mother's sudden vengeful appearance. To make opening night, I had to sleep at a neighbor's house away from her suspicious eyes.

What could have made Mama so fearful? She had joined a strange church that enforced Godly behavior heavy-handedly within its congregation.

Ironically, there was nothing more dramatic than the Saturday morning worship rituals in this church with the leader dressed in pristine starched white delivering 3-hour fire and brimstone sermons. The sermons were not always about God's love for us but an opportunity to scold and vilify the congregation who would shout, roll and tumble throughout the service. The pastor was invited to rebuke me for wanting to be a "brawling woman" the biblical term for someone indecent. My love of theatre caused my excommunication from the church a year later.

It took me four years to get back to the School of Drama. At twenty-one years old, as soon as I could, I signed myself back into acting school and embarked upon a serious career as a professional actor, and enjoyed rave reviews from my peers and critics. Years later, I continued my studies earning a Bachelor of Arts Degree in Theatre Arts and Dance, Acting and Directing. Elliot Eisner says, "The arts have a role to play in refining our sensory system and cultivating our imaginative abilities." Today, my students are the beneficiaries of skills I honed as an actor, director, and playwright. These skills are helping them to expand as critical and creative thinkers. On any given day, I might burst into song to complement their analysis of a literary work or informational text. I might recite a poem about the Harlem Renaissance to refocus my students or cure class fatigue.

Creativity becomes the catalyst that drives industry. Educator and Creativity Expert, Sir. Ken Robinson in his iconic 2006 Ted Talk lecture, viewed, to date, by over 46 million persons across the world, asks one profound question: "Do Schools Kill Creativity?" What unfolds in the next 18 minutes is extraordinary, a critical and compelling argument that examines ways in which parents and schools stymie the creativity of students. He contends that "All kids have tremendous talents. And we squander them, pretty ruthlessly." Robinson tells the heartwarming story of a little girl who was drawing a picture of her imaginative rendering of God. When the teacher challenged the child stating that no one knows what God looks like, the child confidently replied that when she finished her drawing of God the skeptics would know what he looks like. There is no wrong or right. The teacher had a responsibility to honor the child's creativity instead of dismissing her interpretation and trampling on her confidence to imagine the unimaginable.

What happens when the thing we love the most, the thing we believe we were called to do is ripped from us and we are left as vulnerable as a newborn, unplugged from its umbilical life-support? Well, one can turn things around. For me, it meant often sneaking out to see a play or to watch the dance theatre company perform. I am not recommending your children sneak out but what about you? Did you have a personal D-Day? What action did you take to cross the Rubicon?

My mother finally began to thaw after a series of events. The preacher who had presided over my excommunication was a construction engineer. He won the contract and built the new cinema, another so-called den of sin, in the city. The irony wasn't lost on her. She also watched me realize my dream. I was earning money, becoming a responsible young woman. She saw the work in progress, me learning my lines on the verandah. She saw me helping to tell inspiring stories. She eventually came to see me perform in the theatre. I, in turn would forgive my mother for the embarrassment, for saying no and for causing the subsequent loss of my financial scholarship.

I was lucky. I got back in touch with my gift after that close call. What is your gift? Take an inventory to see if an incident from the past had a negative impact and changed your attitude. We unknowingly do the same thing to our children out of fear of hidden dangers or fear of what the neighbors think. Whether it's writing science fiction, or inventing a household tool, find a way to express it. Join a class. Watch how you say 'No' to your children. The future cost could be trust between parent and child. It could also derail the development of a satisfying career and scrub the sparkle from what would be a well-rounded resume. Some of the best lessons you model for of your children are openness and the willingness to change. Silence the voices of naysayers, and create.

Affirmation: *All of creation is a Divine work of art. I am commissioned by the Divine to express my art, and improve my world.*

Chapter 4

Mindfulness

Love the stranger as thyself.

−Leviticus 19:34

New York is truly a garden of cultures, a fusion of centuries-old histories. Manhattan, its centralized hub of entertainment and commerce, attracts people from all around the world. From near and far they have come to build and grow. Yet in this bountiful garden some of us are merely surviving, classed as unwanted weeds, with no healthcare, poor nutrition and lack of a support network. Far too many lack access to the tools to keep them from a hand-to-mouth existence. Some ride the subway day and night because it is their only shelter. Financial challenges are destabilizing the very foundation of their American dream.

Eric, a fourteen year old, lives in a shelter with his parents. The junior high school, two towns away is where he feels a sense of worth and accomplishment. No one, except the Guidance Counselor, knows that he does not live in traditional housing like his peers. Until one day, Eric's classmate, Ng and his local community youth club members entered the shelter laden with clothes and food. For a moment, both Eric and Ng froze and stared at each other till the rest of the club members nudged Ng to step it up so they could get rid of the heavy clothes. A tense Eric eyed the teens as they left. He listened to Ng telling his buddies he would catch up with them. Eric watched Ng approach. He was sure his secret would be exposed at school tomorrow.

"Hey you work here man?"

"No" Eric said and momentarily looked away.

"Yoh, it's cool Eric."

Eric looked at Ng impassively. Understanding crosses Ng's face as he realized Eric lives in the shelter. He digests the situation. "Stuff happens man."

"How come you are here?" Eric asked him.

"My parents told me I have to do community service and lend a hand sometimes."

Eric nodded.

"We good?" Ng asked and held out his fist. Eric hesitated only for a moment. They fist pumped.

"Hey, want to play ball with us at the youth club? We play on Saturday mornings. It's way cool."

"Thanks man. It's been awhile since I played a one-on-one or slam dunk. My parents doesn't want me hanging out in the neighborhood."

"Sounds good to me, man. My parents will drive you back home."

Someone called to Eric and Ng nodded goodbye. Eric watched him walk away and relaxed a little.

Eric had just experienced the village in action - caring about each other and honoring differences. Ng's parents taught him that being mindful of the less fortunate is the right thing to do. Donating money and in-kind goods is wonderful but there is more to giving as well. Ng invites Eric into his circle. Eric is not a leper because of his economic status. On the other side, Eric's parents could be teaching him to lead with trust and not with anger about his circumstances. They could be encouraging him to keep his focus because these are only events, they are not who he is. Benjamin Franklin said, "Having been poor is no shame, but being ashamed of it, is." Eric has to internalize the fact that he has potential to change and shame is the baggage and clutter that needs regular removal. While some find having a chip on the shoulder to be a good motivator, it is still untold stress on the body. Eric doesn't need that. It is better for him to approach life's challenges with the attitude that he has the ability to change his circumstances. This is the vital resilience we need to go through life.

When parents are suffering economically, victim consciousness and feelings of shame are landmines waiting to do away with hope, faith and the energy to work. These feelings make the struggle worse. Many successful people have been down on their luck in the past. A mark of their success was the belief that it was temporary. Leadership coach, Anthony Robbins was on welfare and media mogul Tyler Perry and actress Halle Berry were homeless. Though it is difficult, we can teach our children graciousness whether we are on the giving or receiving end, economically. Eric's mom has him volunteering in the organization's thrift shop. Ng's parents have him dropping off donations. Each one pitches in to help the other. Hard to believe as it may seem, Eric is lucky. For now he has a roof over his head. We don't know how long it will last.

From six years old until graduation from high school, Taliah Connor moved from shelter to shelter, yet credits Hilliard House with helping her pull through and keeping her grades up. Like Eric, she had bad days. She was plagued with anger and fear she would end up in her mother's position. When it was time for homework, the shelter staff helped her walk the line. Her mentor, Miss Peggy, helped her through the college application process. This *Old Dominion University* student considers her experience valuable. She is now grateful to her father for having sent her to live with her mother in the shelter. "I used my mom's experience to see where I didn't want to be."

Major General Linda Singh became homeless but never made it to a shelter. When she was asked how she made it through homelessness. She said, "I slept on the porches of friends' homes or in the back office of the pretzel stand in the Francis Scott Key mall. I made it work." It didn't last for long. She was able to maintain her grades and play Varsity basketball. But it did not last for long. Not surprisingly, "The stress of working, going to school and having no home did me in. My grades declined. I didn't have enough money to take the SAT test. So I dropped out of high school." The US Army was her ticket out of hopelessness.

Life is cyclical and in caring for others, we care for ourselves. Let's raise the happiness quotient. Those of us, who are more fortunate economically and emotionally, may consider reaching out and sharing with those parents in need and by extension, their children. Taliah Connor says living in a homeless shelter is a reality for a lot more people than we realize. "It doesn't mean you're dirty, you're dumb, or you're a drug addict." That was a lot of people when the bubble burst in 2008. You can be a voice for the voiceless, a surrogate for children who struggle academically and socially, a spirit-lifter for those of us in need of hope, a translator for that parent who has no idea what their child is doing in school or a navigator explaining how the school system works. The human garden can only thrive and grow if it is watered with love, fertilized with compassion and access.

Affirmation: *I accept the assignment to show my children how to care for others and themselves in this garden called life. I delight in teaching them to give freely knowing that our abundance comes from a higher source.*

Chapter 5

Never Too Old To Learn

I am defeated, and know it, if I meet any human being from whom I find myself unable to learn anything.

–George Herbert Palmer

I recall purchasing my favorite rabbit ear cellphone. It was trimline and easy to carry around. I wanted it to do everything: unlimited texting, international calling, a high quality camera and endless storage. So without advice, I got the ninety nine dollar full-service plan. I failed to realize that my little rabbit ears cell phone did not have the capacity to give me the comforts of a full-service plan. I paid into that plan for more than a year. In my frustration, I turned to my high school students for advice. Demonstrating technological literacy at its highest level, they explained that I was paying too much for the service. My admiration for these students grew as they delivered an impromptu lecture on efficiency, economics and quality of service. They taught me about myriad feature options: speed, memory expansion, storage capacity, video capabilities, voicemail, style and the best company products on the market. Most of all, they gave me every rational and logical reason why I needed to change with the times and upgrade.

Inspiring stories pulled from today's international headlines prove it's not too old to learn: "90 year old great-great-grandmother, Priscilla Sitienei enrolls in elementary school; 77 year old female bodybuilder Ernestine Shepherd inspires the world with her discipline to stay in shape and lead a healthy life; Eleanor Cunningham does her famous skydiving jump at 100 years old; and Rainelle Burton who was diagnosed with dyslexia and experienced homelessness became an award winning author at 50. How does this happen? These winners have simply said, "I am never too old to learn." There's always room for an upgrade.

Nobody believes in upgrading more than ninety-nine year old Doreetha Daniels. She graduated in 2015 with an AA degree in Social Science from the College of the Canyons. Tired of stained glass painting, ceramics and jewelry, she went back to school in her 90s to do what she dreamt of doing – furthering her education. Things were far different when she tried to get into nursing school in 1935. She never made the cut because she was out-of-state. Instead, she went on to build and nurture her family. Daniels had even more recent losses. At 97 years old, she lost the privilege to drive – that wonderful symbol of American independence. On top of that, she got a stroke while in college. With support and encouragement from children and grandchildren, she got back on her feet and finished her courses. Wise and unflappable she describes her situation:

> "I've had a few bumps in the road, but I have overcome them and finally, June 5th, I'm walking." She tells much younger fellow students "When the bumps come just pick yourself up and say, 'I'm going to go ahead.' And go ahead."

Do you have Doreetha Daniel's strong intent? Spend one Sunday afternoon every quarter at the big library downtown. Add one documentary per month to the family's list. Grandmothers can read a school classic like Franz Kafka's novel *The Fly* and then critique the movie adaptation with your grandchildren. Did the filmmaker do a good job? I remember one mother telling me: O' I don't do the library. I have not had a library card in years." Getting a library card is easy. Why not take your children and a couple of your neighbor's children to become members.

Reading is a joy and it expands the mind. Bill Gates and Warren Buffett read dozens of books per year. Oprah Winfrey started a book club. For those of you who have difficulty leaving home, there are virtual online libraries and museums that you can explore. Take pictures of places of historical value. Cemetery visits may seem a little creepy but you can learn so much about the history of a community by its headstones. Believe it or not, people who happen to be in their second or third career as fantasy authors, get their inspiration from cemetery visits. We live in a time of extraordinary opportunities.

When was the last time you expanded your living geography, whether it is a Segway Tour of your city or a cooking tour of Italy? Taking that much dreamt about trip to Shakespeare's birthplace in England or a literary staycation to New York's Broadway plays does wonders for the soul. A foreign trip might be out of budget but local adventures are easy, free or relatively inexpensive.

Bucket lists are not just for the dying. We should all have a short list of things we want to learn and make every effort to make them fun and execute them. Sit with your children whom you fear have been using the computer as an escape. Don't demonize your children and punish them for being online too much. Let them teach you what they are doing online so you, too, can become a part of the greater world community. Let's get out of our comfort zone and give ourselves permission to learn something new. We too can help our children develop reasoning skills by facilitating discussions about our discoveries and what they are learning about the world. After all, we were their first teacher.

Affirmation: *I am open to learning at every stage of my life. I am open to teaching at every stage of my life. I am present. I am grateful.*

Chapter 6

Courage

Always do what you are afraid to do.

−Ralph Waldo Emerson

My mother was a great swimmer. She loved the ocean so much that from the time she was a young girl, it was a routine for her to swim from one beach to the other on a Sunday. Yet, she never allowed her children to learn to swim. Oh how I yearned to be just like her and there was nothing that could ease this longing. How could a parent raise children on an island caressed by breathtaking ocean scape and not teach or permit her young ones to swim?

I too raised my daughter with a not so healthy dose of fear. When she should have started learning decision making and how to be aware and alert, I still insisted on being the sneaky chaperone at dance classes, bowling, the movies, house parties, you name it. One night, she decided to go to an adult party without my knowledge. Two people got shot. She had been sandwiched between the victims. She almost died. Now, righteous in my fear, I yanked on the reins, I had good reason.

When we moved to Los Angeles, Venice Beach with its explosion of artisans, guys and gals flexing big muscles, beach boardwalk, surfer dudes and great dining – became my place for contemplation and writing. It was a Sunday ritual for my daughter and me. From a safe distance, I would watch her roller skate along the boardwalk beach with reckless abandon and run towards the waves as they rushed to shore. Fear would squeeze my back and shoulders but I never stopped her, I never shouted a warning. I was beginning to realize that as a child, I had been finely tuned to my mother's fearfulness. I had learned to love the ocean from a distance, from the sand, but I still had time to make a change. I was now learning to give my daughter the freedom I never had. I never did give her swimming lessons but when she turned eighteen, I eventually broke the cycle of fear, with her strong encouragement, and granted her freedom to make good decisions for herself. I had to learn to trust again.

There was one more mountain for me to tackle. As time went on, I made several attempts to learn to swim but would build real courage on a visit to Jamaica, thanks to my friend Gloria. At the brush of dawn for an entire week she drove me to the pool and put me in the hands of Kevin, the handsome swim coach. The first time I put my feet in the water, my skin puckered and my body shivered its rejection but I looked over at Kevin whose eyes laughed at my discomfort and at the same time promised trust and protection. 'I've got you.' In that moment, I decided to surrender the fear of drowning. It was not my own. It was something I subscribed to. It belonged to my mother. I slipped into the silky water and lay back into my first float with Kevin's help and the years of yearning fell away.

What had I learnt? Fear and courage are like close relatives, foils of each other. I needed to cultivate courage to learn how to swim. I loved it. I wanted to live a more fun-filled life and swimming was integral to that transformation. I was tired of being the spectator and would wage a campaign to evict the fear that I inherited from my mother. It was a protracted effort. Fear does not give up easily but I was a determined soldier. In the *Battlemind Training* study of soldiers transitioning into home life after war, Carl Andrew Castro, et al., assert that *Battlemind* is the soldier's courage to face fear and adversity during combat. The two components of *Battlemind* are self-confidence and mental toughness; strengths that all soldiers must have to successfully perform in combat.

When next you get a moment for contemplation, reflect upon that thing you want to do, like swimming, but cannot because you are hostage to fear. Act as if you are your parent and write to your childhood self:

Dearest Andrene:

Mama loves you. I know you want to explore the ocean but I am worried I won't be able to keep you safe from the strong currents. When you get older, you are going to learn to swim in a pool. You are going to be the best swimmer ever and perhaps when you have a precious daughter you will understand me just a little bit more and you will also teach her to swim.

Love,

Mama

By putting myself in my mother's shoes, considering the fear she may have felt, and the act of writing it down helped me look at the problem with some objectivity. It helped me to begin to release the anger and accept the healing process. I am reminded of an old saying: If you are to die by drowning you cannot die any other way. However maudlin this translated proverb sounds, it really means that we cannot bend the future to our will. Rather, we should commit to living fully in the moment.

Are you and your children watching from the sand or are you courageously immersing in Life's waters with them? Life throws us challenges and sends us angels like Gloria and Kevin. It is up to us to take their hand and ride the waves or take smaller steps and dangle our feet in the pond.

Affirmation: *In this moment, this fear I feel becomes the diving board from which I jump into the deep sea filled with Life's infinite possibilities. I accept the support already in place for my success. I teach my children how to cope with Life's challenges and setbacks.*

Chapter 7

Love Practice

The state of mind which enables a man to do work of this kind ... is akin to that of the religious worshipper or the lover; the daily effort comes from no deliberate intention or program, but straight from the heart.

–Albert Einstein

Not every baby likes the feel of bath water but we coax them along until they fall in love with it. Going to bed early, eating at a certain time, brushing teeth, the list is endless, we are creatures of habit. The minute we are out of the womb we start creating them. Some habits become destructive like overeating or drug use. On the other hand, some habits give meaning to our lives and when they disappear, they cause unhappiness.

Too often we feel that there is not another minute in the day to do the mundane necessary things men and women do to live much less practice golf swings to qualify for the Golf Channel Amateur Tour. John was at that stage in his life. He had grown up playing golf with his father. Dreams of being a professional first kindled when Tiger Woods won the 2006 PGA Championship. Driven by a powerful emotion, the 17 year-old John never missed a play date with his father. Lack of sleep and exams did not get in the way of him learning distance control and discovering the secret to improving his putting.

When passion met practice, John played five hours per day for most of the week. His game was rewarding. He was beginning to score under par for an average of three out of six games. It took him another four years to build up to this performance level and lower his handicap. His confidence on the green radiated to other areas in his life. Then he got a family and his focus changed. The activity that sparked his passion got compartmentalized in the *Wait! I will get to you soon* closet. He started telling himself, I can only play recreational golf because pro is not for me. Six days of practice soon whittled down to three days and then to the occasional visit to the course. He even stopped watching the majors on television. Over time, coaching his son's Little League Baseball team replaced his golf game while his irons gathered dust in the garage.

When John was playing golf, his son Ryan accompanied him to the golf course and emulated his father's swings, his swagger and his golf talk at home. He would go into the classroom carrying the pride and attitude his father demonstrated. Physical Education class and chess club were at once intense competition and pleasure. In the early grades, the youngster would even remind the teacher about his smiley face reward stickers upon delivering quality homework. Then John transferred his attention to baseball and became the assistant coach of Ryan's Little League team.

Now John had never enjoyed baseball. He hadn't told a soul this but reassured himself it was worth the sacrifice as he loved Ryan and wanted to serve the community. Unfortunately his son was not doing well at the game. Where was the boy who excelled at Phys Ed? Stubbornly, John kept Ryan in baseball and unconsciously became the ugly coach to his seven-year-old boy and other members of the team. His shouts were no longer encouraging. When team members didn't play like he wanted, he would hurl insults at them and tell them they would never play baseball. Ryan got additional scolding in the car on the way home after those games. The once rambunctious and bright boy was now becoming withdrawn. His mother, recognizing the signs threatened to take matters into her own hands and pull Ryan out of baseball. John seemed to be mourning the loss of golf had now started projecting his frustrations on his son. Where are the lines between force and going the extra mile for something you love to do?

Though John didn't realize it at the time, Ryan had offered him the proverbial mirror. He was learning a life lesson from his son. Father and son were both doing an activity they didn't love. John's story gives us an up close view of some of the subtleties at the intersection of creating strong habits and discovering and minding our creative passions. At the positive end of the spectrum is a happier father, a more balanced parent-child relationship and an opportunity to help the child develop habit-building skills to last a lifetime. Some children learn best when they see passion and practice play out in the home.

The old adage says you catch more flies with honey than vinegar. Share that activity you love with your children. It sweetens practice and habit building. Teach by example, letting the children see you throw yourself wholeheartedly into that activity. John hadn't lost his love of golf. He just needed to manage his time. He could have cut back the number of hours on the course, worked with a trainer, found a course nearer home as he continued sharing the game with his son. He could yet get back on the golf course.

Sometimes practice and habit building are a total immersion affair. One need only look at Will Smith's stellar career from teenage rapper to A-List film star and business mogul to see this principle at work. He described his process to the interviewer Rebecca Murray: "I've always considered myself to be just average talent and what I have is a ridiculous insane obsessiveness for practice and preparation."

Smith talks about the opportunity for exchange between parent and child in the rich landscape of learning – the magic that comes as a result of practice and getting in the zone. During the shooting of the film *The Pursuit of Happyness* with his son Jaden, he got stuck during a particular scene, requiring a surprising number of breaks and notes from the director. His son was able to point out that he was emoting in the scene – doing things by rote. Though he was taken aback by it, he turned it over in his mind. By watching his son tackle the same environment naturally and with flexibility and by listening to the director, he was able to make a breakthrough.

Aristotle argues for effective learning by habituation. He believes that "we are what we repeatedly do; excellence is not an act, it is a habit." In some ways, children are grownups in little bodies. What do children love to do? Trust and nurture it. They learn by watching your joy unfold. Then their love and enthusiasm blossoms and grows.

Affirmation: *When I am passionate about something I practice it. When I practice, I am feeding my passion. I easily demonstrate this for my children.*

Chapter 8

Sleep

Take rest; a field that has rested gives a bountiful crop.

–Ovid

When most adults think of rest, they immediately associate it with solitude, inactivity and idleness. When children think of rest, they connect it with boredom. In the 21st Century, it hardly seems that rest is encouraged and we need it now more than any other era. Why? We are bombarded with stimuli from technological advancement and from the world around us. We want it all. We want to respond to it all. We are worn thin and the healthcare industry is hard-pressed to find solutions to our myriad aches and pains. We only need to look at the fatal accidents that occur on the busy highways, on the playing fields, and in our workplaces. According to the National Highway Traffic Safety Administration, driver fatigue is cited as the probable cause of "about 56,000 crashes annually."

As parents, we ought to take serious inventory of the ways in which we treat our bodies and minds. It's a human right – up there with the right to food and freedom. It's a vital need. Our capacity to manage our domestic affairs at home and as a society, let alone international affairs, requires the kind of mind that Lao Tzu speaks of – the one that takes the time out of hectic to be still and watch the universe. Back in my early California days, my Lao Tzu was dance teacher Lady Walquer Vereen. In conversation, she ran the proverbial Sharpie through my over-packed frenetic schedule. Before that I hadn't looked at my schedule of performing and day to day living as something that needed editing. "Andrene, you don't know how to do nothing," she said with so much love and caring. It stayed with me.

Research shows that the brain at rest boosts the immune system and protects our bodies from illnesses. If we do not allow ourselves the opportunity to get enough sleep we are at risk of memory loss, mood swings, poor decision making and the inability to focus on tasks. In the workplace, poor sleep habits lead to poor performance and can eventually bring your integrity under scrutiny and diminish your self-worth.

Here's what sleep accomplishes. The cells of our bodies are rejuvenated and we have a better quality of life. Projects we start are completed and delivered on time. We have enough energy to follow up on your promise to play hide and seek or dodgeball with the children. Our attitude and perception of the world begins to shift and we see the glass half-full and not half-empty and interpersonal relationships improve. It takes energy to reach for success.

It's time to consider changing your sleep patterns and setting some clear goals for your well-being. Like Arianna Huffington says: "Do not take your cellphone to bed with you." Take a break from your electronic devices. Other than controlling the late incoming calls, it has other benefits. The *Harvard Health Letter* reports on groundbreaking research across the country and in Canada on the effects of blue light on the body. Blue light in the sunlight wakes up the body in the morning. At night it's a different story. It blocks the secretion of melatonin and disturbs our natural circadian rhythm.

Harvard researchers and their colleagues conducted an experiment comparing the effects of 6.5 hours of exposure to blue light to exposure to green light of comparable brightness. The blue light suppressed melatonin for about twice as long as the green light and shifted circadian rhythms by twice as much (3 hours vs. 1.5 hours). Blue light emitted from our mobile devices and television screens interfere with quality rest.

During the summer holidays, when I am off from teaching, I usually make it a habit to get a full physical examination and dental checkup. Exercise as often as you can in keeping with the advice of your doctor. According to the Department of Health, your last meal of the day is best eaten at least two hours before bedtime. Liquids should be treated the same way so you don't experience interrupted sleep. Nothing beats a comfortable home environment especially your bedroom that is consciously decorated to your personal taste in furniture, color, smell, and the right type of light for sleep. Read something uplifting before bed. Establish a consistent supportive routine for going to bed.

Let's get some sleep!

Affirmation: *In the stillness I am refreshed, restored, rebuilt, and renewed. My children are healthy because I rest. I am healthy because I rest.*

Chapter 9

Vocabulary For Life

As we express our gratitude, we must never forget that the highest appreciation is not to utter words, but to live by them.

–President John F. Kennedy

Do you remember your schoolyard fights? You were so hurt by your once-upon-a-time friend who lambasted you for some silly misunderstanding. You felt ashamed, unable to find the right words to shut down the taunts. To add insult to injury, a ring of onlookers witnessed your discomfiture. You did everything in your power not to shrink like a mimosa pudica flower. And so you retorted "sticks and stones will break my bones; but words will never harm me." The old adage did the trick. The blush on your cheeks cooled and the supratrochlear vein in your forehead relaxed. I admit I could have used more familiar words to describe the event most of us have experienced. For example, I could have said the frontal vein instead of the supratrochlear, but these are some of the words your children need to learn for their Biology and English tests.

In our world, words rule. Words can have lasting positive effects like those in John F. Kennedy's famous 1961 speech use by countries around the world: "Ask not what your country can do for you; but what you can do for your country." The word is a proverbial weapon in political debates, on the playing fields, in the schoolroom, and in the home. Who can compete with the damaging "Yo Mama" jokes that children use to insult each other?

Superior word knowledge is not reserved only for Spelling Bee champions. We all need it. As a parent, you might be telling yourself, I have been out of school for twenty years and these big and complex words are the last things on my mind. On the other hand, you may have a Ph.D. in History and you may have mastered computer science but need new tools to help you monitor a child's effective acquisition, memorization and recall. Whether it's Biology, English Literature, Chemistry or Calculus, the vocabulary for each subject is unique to the discipline and your child needs to know each for academic interactions, for testing and possibly for a career. Even a 10th grader can still benefit from you whipping out those twenty flashcards, writing the terms on one side, the definition on the reverse and conducting a drill on those hard to learn terms. You proved this method worked when he or she was in elementary school. Don't be afraid to try it again in secondary school.

A student of mine, let's call him Reynaldo for privacy's sake, carried his difficulty with vocabulary through 7th and 8th grade. In my 9th grade high school classroom, he continued to struggle with weekly vocabulary quizzes. The last one devastated the young man. I sensed his agony when he handed me the quiz and shrugged his shoulders in defeat. Determined to help break the cycle, I pulled him aside after class and suggested that he work with his mom during the weekend for the next quiz. I followed up with a call to his mom that afternoon and she was on board.

On the following Monday morning, Reynaldo pushed his way up front and sat next to me. He was excited. Ignoring class protocol he waved his flashcards. He couldn't wait to share his accomplishments and his process of memorization. He wanted to show me that he had the 20 words on one side and the meanings on the other. He was excited that his mother helped him with the new vocabulary. Subsequently, he got a 100% score on the test. Now detractors will say that parents should not play the role of experts or teachers but anecdotal or not, we can't ignore the evidence. Mom still has a role to play with her 9th grader. The march to success began when she decided to drill him at home. Now the scholar is motivated to study with mom for the next test. Yet, his interaction with these new words was not over. His next assignment was to write a creative work of fiction or nonfiction that utilized ten or more words in proper context, demonstrating his understanding of each word. Reynaldo took ownership of the words, not by rote learning but by applying concepts and synthesizing ideas. Ultimately, he published his work, displaying it on the *Students' Writing Wall of Fame*.

    My follow-up note to his mother was one of deep appreciation for her support, helping me to promote independent study and collaboration at home. She did not know these words but was willing to become an active member of the student, parent and teacher team. Mom is learning too and continues to help her child learn how to use words appropriately whether it's for social interaction, success in school or in the work environment. She went back to what was tried and true to get Reynaldo over the hump.

During the 1960s, Betty Hart and Todd Risley compared vocabulary retention in the Turner House Preschool in a poorer Kansas City neighborhood against the children with academic and professional parents. They found that the children in the economically disadvantaged homes had greater difficulty retaining the vocabulary. The study confirmed that language was acquired in the magical 0-3 years. The study also found that all the families observed, whatever their economic status, took good care for their children. The difference was word use – how many times they had heard the persons who shaped their world use the vocabulary. "Simply in words heard, the average child on welfare was having half as much experience per hour (616 words per hour) as the average working-class child (1,251 words per hour) and less than one-third that of the average child in a professional family (2,153 words per hour)." This was the root of the Word Gap phenomenon.

More than half a century later, times have changed. We now have countless children's TV programming and reading campaigns but a gap remains. A child is hardly likely to hear his or her beloved cartoon characters using all the words needed to build a formidable vocabulary. Children imitate their parents. Together, parents and teachers can close the gap. With creativity and hard work, Reynaldo's college dream has a chance of becoming reality. Something is right with the world when you have a hand in helping your child write his or her own compelling and winning college entrance essay.

Affirmation: *Words are fun and I am truly multilingual. I am curious. There are so many opportunities to expand my vocabulary and I take them. I remember words. I had fun teaching my children when they were babies. I can do it again.*

Chapter 10

Secrets Can Harm

I write for those women who do not speak, for those who do not have a voice because they were so terrified, because we are taught to respect fear more than ourselves. We've been taught that silence would save us, but it won't.

–Audre Lorde

Most people of a certain generation grew up being told: Children should be seen and not heard. My father was a different kind of parent. He believed no such thing. You should be seen and heard. If he could not hear us — he would call out to all of us by name. When we arrived, panting and out of breath — he would look us square in the eye, "I don't like when I can't hear you. Now, run along!" Father knew that silence could mean that his children were engaged in some kind of mischief. He also knew silence meant secrets and some secrets can harm.

My silence meant that I was being antisocial, hiding in a corner with a book. Don't get me wrong. He was a teacher and a champion of reading but he knew it was important for me to play and develop social skills. Sometimes we quibble about the noise from children playing on the porch. "Keep it down, out there. Be quiet!" Yet, it is decoding the messages of the noise and the silence that we need to master to understand how our children try to make sense of their world.

What about that once jovial child – the child we were able to read like a book? Are we too exhausted to notice or are we completely absorbed watching our favorite reality show or reruns of our favorite TV show that we forget to engage with this child. That child comes home in silence and disappears into her room. She is not making objectionable noise therefore we relax back into our own world. That child is neither doing homework nor reading a novel; she is carving poems along her arms.

What her parents have missed is the preface to this new phase in her life – it speaks volumes to the dark places she visits in the recesses of her mind. Has she been the victim of bullying or rape? Did we notice the change in behavior but prayed for a miracle or did it slip by us as we worried about the mortgage and credit card bills. Perhaps she has tried to tell adults many times but we are busy and overcome with job stress. Now we must visit her hospital room where she is isolated behind Plexiglas for deliberately harming her body. What secret feeling is being held so deeply that she must harm herself? At the APA's 2006 annual convention in New Orleans, psychologist Sharon Farber discussed the nature of self-harm.

> Self-harm allows the individual to adapt to the most horrific of circumstances without becoming psychotic and without killing himself or someone else, and in that way serves an invaluable defensive function. But it is far more than a defense, and more than a symptom ... It numbs painful affects and protects the patient from fears of annihilation and disintegration.

That secret does not have to be about a real event that was extremely harmful. It could be just a deeply held misconception and oppressive thought she may have about herself.

Let's look at those who keep secrets and then harm others. The high school massacre and suicide in Colorado, teenaged suicide because of cyberbullying and the killing fields at Sandy Hook in Newtown,

Connecticut all happened while parents misinterpreted the gravity of the silence and gave undue space to children who should not be left to their own devices. Some are good at keeping secrets to their detriment. Our children are sadly going to lengths to test boundaries or show they matter.

In an article the *Experience of Secrecy*, Columbia researcher Michael Slepian details his research on the common categories of secrets. He found that 70-80% of persons kept secrets about sexual orientation, lying, cheating at school among other things. Not surprisingly, preference was a key measure on Slepian's study. Preference here means, "not liking something that people think you like, or liking something that people do not know you like." People want to be liked. Our children are no exception.

The good news is, we have a great opportunity to teach our children that it is perfectly normal to enjoy one's personal space but help them to appreciate that parents are responsible for oversight – the kind of oversight that includes monitoring their online activity. Know your child. Though it's likely your children will get mad at you for breaching their personal space, you have to take the risk. Do it with love. A child should never get the opportunity to make a bomb at home or anywhere else for that matter without the knowledge of his or her parents.

Most parents do not see their children off to school with the expectation that they will become vile persons. The majority of teens are not making bombs. Still it takes effort to not be among the few who turn to destruction. We are hardwired with that gut feeling or sixth sense that we sometimes ignore. Harnessing that intuitive power can be the bridge between commonsense and poor judgement, full engagement or leaving the young ones to their own devices.

We were young once. We were sometimes frustrated with our own parents, thinking they were from another planet. Parents sometimes kept their distance. The shoe is now on the other foot. Some teens are notoriously impatient with parents who don't understand their world. We have to break with tradition and have those conversations. In another study Michael Slepian discovered, via participants, that poor judgement came with the act of keeping secrets. "Secrets can be burdensome, affecting how people see and act on the world, with potential negative consequences for physical and mental health."

Slepian's research confirms what we already intuit. In general, revealing secrets whether through telling or writing can "lift that burden." In most cases, parents are protective of their children. Who better to hear a painful secret than a parent? Talking to our children can give us insight into things that matter to them. Creating a safe space for them to share their feelings without fear of judgement helps them build more resilience. If your child comes home unusually hungry chances are someone has taken his or her lunch. I encourage my parents to show up at school, unannounced. Public schools belong to the public. You may be surprised to know that your child has not been going to Math class because a group of bullies has been making his or her life a living nightmare. Take a deep breath. Tune in to the silence. So much is being said.

Affirmation: *I open my heart and my ears to my family and the communities that influence them. I acknowledge my part in our wholeness and lend an ear where I can. I reflect within and listen to my own heart's longing for the parent I never had and the parent I hope to become.*

Chapter 11

Emotional Blackmail

It's a wise father that knows his own child.

−William Shakespeare

Cora was withdrawing from everything she ever loved: softball, the chorale, and the chess club. I remember when she first entered my 9 Honors English class that fall. She was a bright-eyed, lively and intellectually curious youngster who read avidly. There was never a topic she feared to explore. She engaged the class in spirited discourse. Cora is best described as a thinker on roller skates. That year, she made the honor roll in the course with a 97% − pretty good for a girl who worried about her parents divorcing, I thought. Then, at the end of her junior year, the inevitable happened: her parents separated and both she and baby brother were placed in her father's custody.

Her visits to my classroom to say hello became less frequent. The day she brought me her college entrance essay for review and suggestions, I could see her face had lost its polish and she had a new habit: biting her nails. Her illuminating essay was titled: A Pivotal Incident that Changed My Life. She would write:

> That day, my father said, "I thought we were friends. How could you invite your mother to your graduation after she abandoned us? I will not be caught dead in the same room with that woman."

Clearly, both Cora and her father felt some form of betrayal. She, having lost her mother to another man and his children and her dad's discovery that Cora was secretly communicating with his foe of an ex-wife. What is a child supposed to do now that her father has decided to boycott her graduation? The essay continues:

> In that moment, something shifted inside of me and I got this big nudge that if I make this day about my parents, I will miss its significance and power to guide my future. I uninvited my mother and father and invited my younger brother, instead.

What Cora's father did not realize was that he had wounded his adolescent daughter with the emotional darts that pierced his own heart. All Cora wanted to be was a good daughter and student. Instead, her father had emotionally blackmailed her. Was this fair to boycott her graduation? On her biggest day, neither parent was there to celebrate with her. Psychologist Susan Forward says, "Perhaps worst of all, every time we capitulate to emotional blackmail, we lose contact with our integrity, the inner compass that helps us determine what our values and behavior should be." She goes on to say that though it's not, "heavy-duty abuse, don't think for a moment that the stakes aren't high." In other words, it's highly likely that Cora will take this into adulthood.

Life happens. Homes are constantly being disrupted as adults navigate in and out of relationships. Children are often the biggest casualties. Seen from their viewpoint, they are losing the very foundation that keeps them grounded and safe. Their whole world is crumbling and they do not know how to fit the pieces back together. Nothing makes sense in their new world. This radical shift that makes them responsible for the happiness of their parents is mind-blowing, life-altering and off-putting. They are ill-equipped for this role reversal.

What can we do to make it better for our children? Children of divorce feel abandoned. Their deepest challenge is to remain uninjured by that abandonment. The American Academy of Child and Adolescent Psychiatry (AACAP) offers tips on how parents should really behave with children during a divorce. Among the tips:

- Do not keep it a secret or wait till the last minute
- Tell them the divorce is not their fault
- Do not discuss each other's faults or problems with the child

Instead as the AACAP advises, "Parents should be alert to signs of distress in their children. Young children may react to the divorce by becoming aggressive and uncooperative or by withdrawing. Older children may feel deep sadness and loss."

Cora's father forced her to make grown-up pacts. Fortunately, the writing assignment proved to be a decompression tool for Cora. Her choosing to focus on this intimate topic in her essay gives us hope. She is not burying it in the subconscious mind. Some children are not so emotionally developed. Be mindful of using our children as weapons in fighting adult emotional warfare.

Affirmation: *In this moment, I acknowledge my humanness. I forgive those who hurt me. I am able to see things from my children's point of view. I love my children unconditionally.*

Chapter 12

Failure

Failure and success are first cousins working together for my good.

−Andrene Bonner

Failure is not an option! For years, this was the mantra I chanted to my students after presenting the syllabus at the beginning of every school year. They knew right away that my expectations, and by extension that of the English Department and the school is that they have to succeed. Then one day the quiet inner question followed: Is it really? What is failure and whose failure are you talking about? I had bought into the popular but sometimes erroneous belief that as a teacher I was responsible for my students' failure.

Oftentimes, I would say to my students, your report card is my report card − it's not all about you! Ego Alert! I was projecting my own fear about punishment that I took with me from my own childhood. This fear had put me in an emotional straitjacket as a young member of Tribe Bonner and a student of the Jamaican school system, at the time, built purely on scholarship and reward. Helped by the demands of the American school system's paralyzing teacher assessment strategies, I had taken this fear into the classroom.

Failure and Success are cousins – the classic co-conspirators activating our purpose. How we look at failed or failing events in our lives activates the success code sequences in our DNA. We only need to look at some of the world's most successful moguls who attribute their achievements in life to failed projects. Oprah Winfrey was fired from her job as a news anchor only to later revolutionize television and book publishing.

Early in his career, Walt Disney failed to impress as an imaginative mind but created iconic cartoon characters, Disney Studios and won the Nobel Prize. Albert Einstein was not regarded as a rising star in school but his theory of relativity transformed the way we approach the study of physical science. Bill Gates failed at his first business venture Traf-O-Data and dropped out of Harvard University before Microsoft dominated the information technology age. Tyler Perry speaks often of his homelessness and failed projects and is one of today's quintessential storytellers whose works dominate the stage and film.

These successful leaders had one important habit. They looked at failure as a wayshower of sorts, an invitation to change course, to make adjustments however small or large – a chance to add a new step to their current strategy. In class, my epiphany was a catalyst to reflect, relearn and revise my lessons making them more accessible to students with diverse learning styles. In Perry's world failure gave him the focus to develop his writing and become more finely tuned to what would appeal to his potential audience.

So necessary is the need to look at failure with new lens that Smith College has established a project allowing students and faculty to publicly talk about their worst failures. Rachel Simmons, a leadership development specialist at Smith, developed the series and reports the goal of the experiment is to help students develop resilience. "The Failing Well series gives students tools for rethinking failures and managing achievement related pressure." Simmons' own failure resume describes her setback dropping out of the Rhodes Scholarship Program. Her lesson: "Stop pursuing achievements because they pleased others and made me look good ..." Students are already reporting a change in attitude. One called it "positive therapy" and another says, "When one door closes, another opens."

As young children, our family and environment helped form our definitions of failure. They had far reaching effects from our performance in school through career. Often creativity and resilience are at the mercy of this constricted definition. Nurture that little entrepreneur who didn't sell much at the lemonade stand. Where could that child make adjustments? Does it require a change in product or location? Encourage him or her to come back next summer and succeed selling icies. Your daughter – the one who makes cookies and raises money for the homeless program at your church, may need to tweak her script if her previous approach didn't win over buyers. Then there is the little scientist in your son who pulls apart every electronic gadget, studies them, and then puts them back together only to have them fail to work. Help turn his frustration into fun exploration. Redefine failure for your children and rekindle their curiosity.

If, as a parent, you don't feel an affinity for that area of interest your child has, get help. Certainly if you didn't get those opportunities with your parents, then you would be breaking the cycle. Ultimately, it's an opportunity to create a reasonable working area for them to explore, create and grow. Take the fear out of learning. Speak positively into their lives those words that encourage your children's success. As the parent and teacher in the home, with your waking hours fully taxed, try anyway to carve out some time to study and play with them. Through your children, a whole new world of learning will open to you and together everyone will enjoy success!

Affirmation: *In this very classroom of life, I open myself to accept that failure and success are working together for my good and that of my children. I am successful. My children are successful.*

Chapter 13

Grief

We build too many walls and not enough bridges.

–Isaac Newton

Becky has been grieving for her son Ethan for eleven years. She would light candles, pray and weep for days on end at the altar of photos, baseball cards, comics and items of clothing. Her tears turned into poor eating habits, to the point of starvation. She was emotionally and physically ill. She looked wretched. Thirteen year-old Ethan was shot and killed outside the family home. He was returning home from the corner store with a small bag of groceries she had asked him to purchase when he was showered with a hail of bullets at the safety of his gate. Her guilt and grief knew no bounds. "It is all my fault!" Becky could hardly accept that she was outliving her son.

The Centers for Disease Control and Prevention report that "In 2010, 4,678 young people were homicide victims. This translates into everyday 13 young people in this country are murdered." Ethan was among those young people. Becky was ravaged by the loss. Something equally devastating was happening elsewhere in Becky's home. Her husband, Bill and ten year old daughter, Anna no longer existed. Becky stopped taking care of her daughter. Throughout Anna's high school years, all the day-to-day management and important decisions fell to Bill.

Despite the crisis, father and daughter achieved little triumphs along the way. His daughter had become an outstanding scholar and earned multiple scholarships to college. Bill did everything in his power from getting full-time homecare to providing the best mental health counselor for Becky. Anna would encourage her to leave the house and spend quality time outside and get some fresh air. Even then, she would sit and dream about Ethan playing in the garden. She would tell stories as if he was still alive – as if he was still thirteen.

One Saturday, as Becky dozed on Ethan's bed, a candle from her makeshift altar toppled over and created a wall of fire near the window. Her husband's voice raised the alarm elsewhere in the house, "Becky,

Anna, Fire!" as smoke filled, slid and snaked around the furniture and into the ceiling, choking the house with haze. The flames quickly spread. If Martin hadn't been home it would be a different story. He managed to hustle everyone out. They coughed uncontrollably as they made their escape. As the firemen battled the flames which had now enveloped half the house, Becky looked on in shock at the destruction of their home and the pain in her husband's eyes. Anna was clearly hurting too. How had things gotten so bad?

It's been five years since the fire. Becky no longer needs a nurse but participates in a support group and gets additional counseling. Anna has graduated from college and is now planning a family. Since Becky was emotionally unavailable to her during high school and missed the celebrations of her many milestones, Anna got counseling as well. She was determined to not have the wounded child dominate her life. Both Becky and Anna are lucky. Bill and Becky grew apart as husband and wife but have remained friends. Bill himself attends a support group and is recuperating from Ethan's death. Together, they can find ways to celebrate Ethan and live meaningfully.

How long should we mourn? How high and wide should we build our wall of sadness? No one dares to answer for the other. As each of us is unique, so is our process of grieving. There is no quick fix, but there is process. Seek professional counsel. Psychiatrist Elisabeth Kübler-Ross, after a landmark study of terminally ill patients, sets the measurement for the study and treatment of grief. In the book *On Death and Dying,* she describes five stages of grief: denial, anger, bargaining, depression, and acceptance. Retrofit these stages over Becky's loss and we find her clearly stuck in the "Denial" stage. The fire, as unfortunate as it is, catapulted her out of her near catatonic state.

Kubler-Ross in her 2005 expansion on the first book, *Finding the Meaning of Grief Through the Five Stages of Loss,* says, "As the denial fades, it is slowly replaced with the reality of the loss. You begin to question the how and the why." Becky isn't out of the woods yet. She has put on a little weight and is in and out of anger and asking God why he hadn't done anything to save Ethan. It is a good sign. At least she is not wishing she were dead.

We need alone time to surrender and be present with grief. That may mean a family member or friend babysitting. But when we have children we have to find ways to help them to grieve as well. We need language for that role. Here's where professional counsel comes in. It is essential we keep our vulnerable children and loved ones at the center of our world. Talk to friends who are good listeners. Join a group for people who have suffered a similar loss.

Learning the practice of meditation might be just the tool to quiet the unbearable chatter in your head. Journaling has the advantage of dumping your feeling on the page and easing the pressure. We will suffer very painful loss. We will mourn. It's difficult for children to stare at the walls of our hopelessness and thrive. Wellness of those children left behind – matters.

Affirmation: *Dear Divine. I don't know why (insert loved one's name here) is gone. This pain I feel confirms that I know the value of life and I have the capacity to love. Thank you for breath and life. Thank you for the gift of resilience and your divine love. I want to make the most of it.*

Chapter 14

Guiding Teens

As long as you live, keep learning how to live.

−Seneca

Dr. Brené Brown cites shame as "The most powerful, master emotion. It's the fear that we're not good enough." She contends that it is most "destructive" because it grows exponentially in our lives through "secrecy, silence and judgement."

Mina and Bob are two hard-working parents living in the suburbs of Westchester and run a business together in the town. They are convinced that there is nothing more they can do about their son, Lyle. The tween has fallen in with the wrong crowd and is on a downward spiral with 'No Good' written all over it. His grades are the same. Mina and Bob tried everything: telling him off about his worthlessness, punishment and counseling. Nothing worked and they were terrified they would lose him. They felt ashamed.

Things came to a head one day with both parents throwing accusations at each other. Then came Mina's revelation. "You were selling nickel bags of marijuana in college. You had your brush with the law. So why don't you try to help your son," Mina yelled.

Bob's voice dropped, "Don't you think that's what I'm doing? Mina the boy is hopeless."

"How can you say that?"

"I changed because I saw you and my career in my future. The boy has no ambition!"

"The neighbors are talking. The family is talking. What next? The people at our workplaces will be talking! Don't you care about that, Bob?" Mina's indignation made the other children come rushing to the top of the redwood stairs. "What about them, Bob. What about them?"

Bob glanced quickly at the children. Had they heard Mina talk about his brush with the law? He gazed at Mina, his eyes begging her to be quiet.

"The others will turn out right." He picked up the Wall Street Journal.

Bob was once a troubled teen. There are two ways he can look upon his past: as a shameful secret or as an inspirational example for Lyle. He transformed himself into a responsible father but refuses to look at the similarities between himself and his son. Lyle and his teenaged peers are testing their boundaries. The first strategy is for Bob and Mina to dig a little deeper – go within. Digging deeper brings objectivity. It helps parents make peace with the past. Digging deeper brings clarity – a dialing down on the shame, judgement and anger. Those emotions are conversation busters within the family. We see it happening as Mina berates Bob in front of the children. This is a confrontation with Bob when they both should, with helpful tools and love, confront the past together.

The second is for Bob to be honest with Lyle about his own history as a troubled teen and the worry he experiences when thinking about Lyle's future. Bob has to discuss his own transformation with the young man and send a powerful message. He should be able to describe the turning points and the important lessons he learned from his past experiences. In addition, they should be honest with Lyle about the real effect of his behavior on the family. Embarrassing nosey neighbors and critical family are the least important reason for needing to discipline a teen.

Third, getting outside help may be necessary to conduct that difficult conversation and to facilitate change. Mina wants Bob to be the authority figure but Bob may not be equipped to have that conversation with Lyle. He may be a poor listener. He may have inherited his parenting style from his own parents. His dad probably hid behind the newspaper at the first sign of trouble and left the brokering to Mom.

Depending on the level of disruption in the home, Lyle may need a change in environment. Some experts recommend youth intervention services. However, leaving home should be the last resort. My father, a strategic thinker, welcomed select friends into our home. That's the only way he could tell the type of characters within his children's peer groups. Teens need a break from peer pressure. My mom popped in at school when necessary. She did not have to be invited. This kept us on our toes.

Providing guidance to teens is tough business and requires hardcore critical thinking and at times unorthodox parenting skills. It requires a change from what parents do for much younger kids. Be creative with the tools you have. In its checklist *Communication Tips for Parents*, the American Psychological Association suggest "soften strong reactions; kids will tune you out if you appear angry or defensive." The second item on the checklist says, "Express your opinion without putting down theirs; acknowledge that it's okay to disagree." Remember, we were once at the teenage stage, feeling the same angst. Be firm, be creative but above all, approach with empathy.

In the character bible, *Please Understand Me II*, Psychologist David Keirsey takes it a step further. He says, "From the beginning children are very much their own persons." Like adults, they can belong to any one of the four groups: Artisans, Guardians, Idealists and Rationals. His sketch of the artisan child is an eye-opener. This child has punctuality and organization issues. He or she gets excited quickly but gets easily bored too and into mischief. Since the artisan child is going to push the limits and experiment, it's necessary to set boundaries early for that child without tamping down on his or her creativity. If Lyle is an artisan teen, giving him outlets for his creativity and what Keirsey calls "impulsiveness and insubordination" goes a long way to keeping him out of trouble and makes communication easier. If he's now accused of being too impulsive and insubordinate, it's not a winning argument and will not necessarily change behavior.

The idea is to consider the teen's personality as you consider intervention. Drug addiction is no trivial matter. Lyle's bad behavior could be a cry for help and just finding out what irks him may be all Mina and Bob need to know to help him find balance and confidence. Telling him he is worthless is counterproductive. Punishing him for the same behavior dad did earlier in life is plain hypocritical. Teens will find their way through the labyrinth of fear, awkwardness and anger and come back to the fold, if we are present to show them that their stumbling blocks are stepping stones to success.

Affirmation: *I acknowledge the beauty of youth. I accept my responsibility to nurture and create a safe place for my children's exploration and growth. I have the wisdom to know when hard truths are necessary. I am honest about the mistakes of my past and hope it's an inspiration to others.*

Chapter 15

Gratitude

Be content with what you have; rejoice in the way things are. When you realize there is nothing lacking, the whole world belongs to you.

—Lao Tzu

King Grisly-Beard is a story by Brothers Grimm about the princess who was forced to marry a dirty looking fiddler. The princess was living a lavish life in the palace and she mocked and rejected the finest and noblest young princes who dared to propose to her. Her father, the King, believed that she was too arrogant and ungrateful, and so he schemed to have her marry a beggar who happened to be a fine fiddler. In her new arranged life, the princess eked out an existence in poverty and servitude with the fiddler until she learnt her lesson.

As fairytales go, the solution is drastic and the ending happy. The fiddler was, after all, a nobleman. However, it is the lessons that stay with us – in her case: be grateful and never take anything for granted. She learned respect for the feelings of others. She learned to appreciate even the mundane: harvesting her own food, washing, cooking and cleaning. She tapped into her own creativity as a weaver and became an entrepreneur by selling those baskets.

Demonstrating gratitude is not a one-size-fits-all set of strategies. The more creative the better. But there is universality too. For starters, just a simple thank you to someone who opened a door or helped you with the groceries to your car. Practice telling your children thank you for doing chores around the house. Let them know that you value their contributions to making the load lighter. I know many of us do this already but it bears repetition. If you model gratitude it becomes a habit for them and in time it becomes their nature.

What of our attitude about our so-called unfortunate circumstances? Hindsight is worth gold. I support the idea of Gratitude Journaling made popular by Sarah Breathnach and Oprah Winfrey. When I journal, it keeps me grounded whenever I feel overwhelmed by a current problem especially those I drag from my past into the present. The act of writing in the journal gives me some objectivity and centers me. Then I am able to see the problem as an opportunity. But the journal also gives me a telescopic view of the distant past.

Trials and tribulations transformed the princess, giving her fortitude and skills she otherwise would not have learnt in the palace. She has to be thankful for the whole lot, not just the harvest but the pain of gardening, the broken nail, being pricked by thorns, tilling the soil early in the morning when all was asleep, working when it was cold, the journey to market and so on. My journaling has put things in perspective in much the same way for me.

Vulnerability expert and research professor at the University of Houston, Dr. Brené Brown shares her findings that "Actively practicing gratitude invites joy into our lives." As parents, we can be thankful that we have been chosen as change agents in our home, in our workplace and in the larger society. Don't wait till you have to be as drastic as King Grisly Beard to teach your children how to live gratefully. Do it now. Thank someone for being a wonderful and significant presence in your life. Should you ever feel the urge to measure your children against their siblings and your neighbor's children, turn that impulse into a gratitude moment – a moment to be thankful for the wonderful children who are as diverse as the planets.

Encourage children to try journaling daily or weekly by writing at least two reasons to be grateful. It improves their writing skills and their self-expression and it doesn't have to be writing, it can be doodles or drawings. You will be amazed what you learn about them. Journaling keeps the conversations going between parents and children. What a wonderful way to tell each other simply: Thank You!

Affirmation: *I am grateful for my teachers. I am grateful for the opportunity to give and receive love. I enjoy teaching my children how to be grateful.*

Chapter 16

Intention

Our intention creates our reality.

−Wayne Dyer

I didn't mean to. We hear this statement over and over again, usually, because it comes after a particular action and its undesirable outcomes. Whether positive or negative, intention is part of the foundation resulting in scientific breakthroughs, inventions, political campaigns, great books, enduring and masterful poetry. They are all results of creative intentions, purposes or aims people hold in their hearts and minds.

I have been meditating on this book through my thoughts, actions and my work for more than forty years. My intention is a kind of pre-meditation, a prayer with an end in mind. As a child, I saw my dad teaching adults to read from books I was using in school. I witnessed their eyes lighting up as they entered new territories of understanding. This fascinated me so much. I dreamed of doing the same. I did not have all the tools back then, but I had intention. I began writing and the intention was set in motion.

It is my experience that when I set an intention, it has to be clear or else I end up circling like a plane in a holding pattern, unable to land. Intentions are never static. An intention is a living energy force always there to be acted upon to keep our goals alive. As a child, I made books by taking my father's typewriting paper, fold them in half, write stories and draw pictures on them. Then I would bind them with a pin. This way, my dolls and pets would have something to read. Dad and mom always encouraged me to write. Then there were the many teachers of my youth and now there are those in my adult life I call professor, family, mentor and friend. Every step of the way, I was getting help although often unaware. The manifestation of this book is an example of intention in motion to achieve the goal of authorship.

In a PBS article, *How Intention Can Make You Learn Better*, writer Annie Murphy Paul does a survey of new learning strategies in listening. According to her report, studies in Canada and China are proving scientifically that students can simply observe with intentionality and achieve high performance results. University of Ottawa language researcher, Professor Larry Vandergrift proved the theory with students learning French as a second language.

> "Skilled learners go into a listening session with a sense of what they want to get out of it. They set a goal for their listening, and they generate predictions about what the speaker will say. Before the talking begins, they mentally review what they already know about the subject, and form an intention to "listen out for" what's important or relevant."

Paul's article shows that learning with intentionality is not limited to listening. Dancers achieve the same results when they watch and dissect the dance routines of other dancers. Behavior change gurus have been talking about intention for eons.

There is an old saying that the road to hell is paved with good intentions. I will replace "hell" with "success." In that I mean, a good intention is a gut feeling you have that stays with you and tells you that one day you will grow mangoes on the moon. Yet, at times, we have every intention of attaining our well-thought out goals that we set for ourselves but snags in the road have a way of veering us off course.

My daughter often tells me to just trust the process when I get too concerned about my desired outcome in a lesson unit or just the overall welfare of a student who does not seem to be applying himself or herself. She reminds me that my steps to attain my goals have been carefully planned and that my good intentions will drive the machinery.

Have you had an unrealized goal for a long time? Did you set a clear intention to propel that goal to fruition? If the answer is no, then it is time to take inventory. Make an evaluation. Read books on goal setting and intention. You may find some clues as to why the goal hasn't manifested. In *The Four Desires*, Rod Stryker says, "Transmitting your intention from the calm of prayer or meditation endows that intention with the most power and thus allows you to have the most influence on the material world." Be meticulous and look for answers from your childhood. Interview someone whose achievements you have admired from afar. Ask them how they got to their goal.

Some manifestations may take a month to be realized and others may take forty years or more, but see them happening as you desire. Further, break them down into manageable pieces whether by time, by deliverables or both. Elon Musk created *SpaceX* because he wanted to go to Mars. Will he go to Mars in this lifetime? Should we even ask that question? Some people have called him genius. Others think he is insane. Yet strong intention has Musk now shipping cargo to the space station via his rocket company *SpaceX* on behalf of NASA. Hiring contractors to fly on its behalf was not a dream of NASA when it first went to the moon yet here we are.

Set your intention. My intention is to be a highly effective teacher and so I set two types of goals: My personal and students' goals. These goals are long term and short term – a school year versus five years. How do I plan to get there? I can attend some professional development workshops with the masters in curriculum design and innovation. For my five year goal, I may plan on going to Africa and set up a program in a rural area in technological literacy.

Parents can do long term planning as well. Any number of events can threaten to railroad acting on an intention. Consider as many of these unexpected events in your planning. Some parents have set ambitious reading goals for children and have achieved them – reading fifty-two books per year. Warren Buffett, Elon

Musk, Oprah Winfrey are avid readers. You can do likewise. If you desire to improve your finances so that you and your children can afford to have a home library, start saving early. If funds are slim, use the local library.

Tired of being a tenant? Then set a goal to become a homeowner and plan the steps to doing so. Read all you can find on homeownership. Go to seminars in your area. They are listed in your free circulars in your local supermarket. Find organizations that can educate you on your credit score. Let your children share in this experience so they will appreciate the value of saving and investing in something the family desires. They will be subscribing to intentions mutually beneficial to the entire family.

Affirmation: *I call into my life good intentions that fuel my goals for success. I teach my children how to set goals and they are successful.*

Chapter 17

People Pleasing

All of us wish we'd had perfect childhoods, with a mother and father who modeled ideal parental attitudes and taught us to internalize the tenets of self-love. Many of us, however, did not.

—Marianne Williamson

Oftentimes, we give to others so much that there is nothing left to give to ourselves because we are hiding a world of hurt under our turtle-shell like exterior.

Just about anybody she called friend feeds off the sweet nectar oozing from her heart. Celine knew how to throw a party: four, sometimes six in a year flowing with potent pleasure drinks and food. Nothing pleased her more than to see everyone happy, even when the whole weekend was dedicated to planning and she is left to clean up at 4 a.m., with only two hours to get a nap before work. Here was a woman who was intent on creating for her guests what she could not do for herself.

Celine was unhappy. She secretly hated her job. At work she willingly accepted the next project even if it was not a part of her job description – filling what should be her me-time with their-time. More often than not, she labored without a thank you. She hated that her man only sought intimacy when he felt like it and hid from her the rest of the time. They shared nothing of the heart, nothing intellectually stimulating. Celine had seen her parents do the same painful thing. They were poor and had stayed together out of convenience even though they fought all the time.

Wanting to break the cycle of poverty she made sure to take advantage of the best public school education offered her. After graduation, she got a job on Park Avenue that allowed her to go to college part-time and she would stay in it long enough to get the kind of salary that afforded her a big house in the suburbs, nice car and two poodles. This was the security she believed she needed. Her self-worth was linked to the value her friends placed on her. The parties did just that. Sadly, no one taught her how to love herself. No one modeled for her in her formative years that she is not the external trappings but a decent, well-intentioned human being inside.

One day, I got the courage to ask her: How are you really doing? She said, "I don't know. I really don't." In that moment, her vulnerability burst through her pores. Tears flowed down her face. I believe this was a moment of truth for her. We sat there for some minutes as she courageously faced the pain. The following weekend, I introduced her to my dog-eared copy of Dr. Don Miguel Ruiz's brilliant book: *The Four Agreements*. In it, he shares four salient strategies that get to the root of our choices and the sufferings that we must eventually use to springboard us to our own self-healing. Of course Celine was reluctant at first to accept the teachings.

Weeks following, she shared that she had really latched onto Agreement Number Four: *Do Not Make Assumptions*. Celine was beginning to understand that clear communication was central to good relationships whether with our friends, workplace or a lover. Over time she built up the courage to speak up for herself when her non-committed partner wanted to visit. She started saying what she expected in a relationship. Celine loved to entertain but over time, she got kinder to herself regarding those glittery all-nighters at her house. She cut down on the number of parties and hired a tiny team to help her cleanup. She lost some people from her circle but also began to build more enriching friendships.

Are we giving to others so much that there is nothing left for us? Are we hiding a world of hurt under a smiling exterior? Now is the perfect time to ask ourselves if our actions are tied to people pleasing. Do you feel guilty about saying no – this is hurting me, this is not serving me well? Start saying no to projects that cut into your me-time. Set those boundaries. Stop feeding the fear of loneliness. Being in your own company can open up new vistas. You might get the same opportunity to self-examine as Celine did. You might just write that cookbook filled with recipes from your late mother, start a quilting club with the ladies on your block or join a Salsa dance class. Start chipping away at that turtle-shell, that protective shield that is locking you away from the sunlight of your success. Let your children see your true smile. Let them see you loving what you do, loving yourself, rewarding yourself. Pretty soon, your house will be filled with life affirming attitude. Let's sweep away the dust and the footprints of those who walk all over our dignity. Let's serve from a place of wholeness.

Affirmation: *I am created in the image I am meant to be. I am worthy. I am a reflection of that light the world needs to see.*

Chapter 18

Forgiveness

You are the bows from which your children as living arrows are sent forth.

–Khalil Gibran

What happens when a father is absent from a child's life because of work, incarceration, warfare, fecklessness or even death? Do we expect that child to understand fully the magnitude of the absence or do we ignore it in the hope that one day the child who is left behind will be well?

As I contemplated this principle, I was drawn to my favorite Hollywood dad and storyteller: Steven Spielberg. He tells the story of his father's workaholism that destabilized the family home and put a wedge between them for years. When Steven himself became a father, his storytelling shifted and put the spotlight on the effects of the absent father on children. He finally began to heal that rift. The story ends well as the filmmaker eventually reconciled with his dad. Like Spielberg, I loved my father dearly but wrestled with his absence for a very long time. My father died when I was only 16 in the midst of my high school final examinations at the brush of entering university. It shifted my world.

For a long time, I regarded my father dying and leaving me and my siblings to navigate uncharted waters of life with a mixture of love and anger. He left us with no compass, I thought. Psychotherapists and grief counselors weren't a regular offering in our culture; at least, I did not know how to access it. My school leaders couldn't help. My church leaders did no hands-on work. Instead, some just prayed. Other church members, who had been his colleagues in ministry, abused us.

Now that there was no protector in the home, we were bullied by a family across the street. There was an endless list of woes. Mama, left to raise four school age children on her own, immediately enlisted God and my older sister as surrogate parents. My sister, Antonette, only nineteen years old, working and attending college, was drafted to help raise the family – it meant she suddenly had to worry about fares to ride the bus, lunch, clothing, rent, the list goes on. She made the sacrifice. We were bereft. How could he leave us so soon?

During my early adult life, every time I fell upon hard times or I had near ruinous fallout with a lover, I blamed Dada. I held the dead man accountable for everything that I could not fix. You see, when I was a child, my dad could fix anything: from a broken shoe heel to my measles-scarred skin. Dada could soothe any sadness. There was no one like him around to quell the pain. For years, I was stuck at sixteen with a hole in my heart that no one could fill.

As I was writing the book, I continued to pore over what it means to wake up one day with your parent gone. Then the epiphany – for the first time, my memory of Egbert Bonner wasn't tinged with anger. I wasn't thinking of myself as the victim nursing my wounds of abandonment. I was thinking of how amazing he was a father. Soon I was quizzing my brother about some of Dada's memorable quotations. We had belly laughs like children as we shouted out his hilarious and sarcastic one-liners. Suddenly there was no sadness, only love between us three: my father – in spirit, my brother and me. This was more than an issue of forgiveness. After all Dada had done nothing wrong. The Divine had created the perfect opportunity for me to acknowledge and release the anger.

Losing a parent leaves its mark on a child, whether the loss is from death, separation or even workaholism. What can we do as parents to heal that void? Given circumstances, environment and personality must dictate. As adults, we can help the younger ones make sense of the kind of absence they are experiencing. Some military personnel never return from the field. They die while serving. But those fathers, who return from service, are missed just as keenly as if they had passed away while in the field. We have seen the videos of soldiers on leave, surprising their kids. It brings tears to the eyes. Mom can tell her children he's gone to serve and protect and he's coming back. Communication from Dad while he is in the field helps maintain the parent-child emotional connection.

Healing the void created by temporary absence does not mean we anesthetize the children. When the other parent is absent or in the war zone, some parents may find themselves trying to shield their children from the horrors of war by choosing instead play fun games or watch light-hearted television show. Yet today's children are connected to communities of their peers all over the world on consoles playing violent war games. It should not be total emersion in violence their every waking moment. In this day and age, terror attacks and the immediacy of social media reports are creating a lot of anxiety in our children. Some of my students refuse to engage in discussions about 9-11 that devastated the lives of our citizen and ushered in a new way of existence. I understand fully their trepidation. Children have impressionable minds. They should not watch back to back cycles of the same violent news. It compounds the stress felt from the loved one who is absent.

Losing a parent through divorce delivers its own emotional setbacks. The rate of divorce in the US is startling and unfortunately children are one of its casualties. The National Center for Health Statistics in a 2013 report states that only 45% of fathers aged 15-44 were living with their children, biological, adopted or otherwise. Some of the remaining 55% can be attributed to divorce. Numbers show that some of those divorces likely happened while the children were preteen – a delicate stage of development. You may have children who are developing at different stages and the responses to life at each stage are unique.

When my daughter's father decided to create a new family with someone else, I tried to protect my daughter from the monster called the break-up. How I behaved in front of her was appropriate for the most part. In hindsight, my reactions created their own problems. I was not successful in shielding her from my tears. I tried to hide it but she knew and was greatly affected by it. Dad was missing and I was essentially in mourning. I know it is not easy to be our best selves in front of our children during these times. Seek professional counsel.

What if I had lost Dada at eleven years old? It happened to my brother. At that age he had less emotional ability or even the freedom to grieve the loss. It is only now as adults that my siblings and I speak about these feelings and not everyone wants to go there. Some are unwilling to talk about the hurt caused by his death and our family life after his passing. So that hurt, stays locked inside, silently building walls, undermining our confidence and or creating emotional mayhem. We can't ignore the effects of the absent father in the hope that one day the one left behind will be well. Don't assume your children are okay. It's time to become the emotional police and check in on them. It's not too late to chart a plan in your adult years to break the tyranny of the past, help our children build resilience and prepare for success.

Affirmation: *My life is a connection of events that are guided by the power of the ancestors. I bless Dada's spirit for the gifts of love and forgiveness. I bless Mom and my sister for lifting up the mantle and filling in when he could no longer carry it. I am a blessing to children who experience loss and who come under my influence.*

Chapter 19

Love Letters

It is the writer who might catch the imagination of young people, and plant a seed that will flower and come to fruition.

—Isaac Asimov

Love and food are brain fuels from the gods and unconditional love is healthy for the giver as it is for the receiver. While some people are afraid to be vulnerable in demonstrating expressions of love, others simply do not know how because it was never modeled for them.

My sister Sandra knows and practices these principles so well through her inspirational writings, life affirming love notes to her daughters. She sends love notes in their lunch boxes of specially prepared eats, a tradition she has held dear from the first day her girls entered Kindergarten. Today, her youngest is away in college but mom's love-texts fuel her days, while the oldest, a New York City schoolteacher enjoys mom's love notes posted to her lunch bag, a pleasant reminder that a mother's love has no age limit. On a rainy New York morning, San would write something like this:

> It is raining outside;
> but inside your heart
> it is fuzzy and warm.

Imagine what this does to an impressionable six year old let alone a young adult. It makes me wonder what goes through a child's mind in that moment the torrents banging against the school windows bring on a rush of fear: "I want my mommy!" Suddenly, mommy shows up on a Post-It Love Note that just calms the fears and warms the heart. At other times, she would evoke the classic Henry Wadsworth Longfellow of her childhood gems after they stayed up past bedtime to complete their science project:

> The heights by great men reached and kept
> were not attained by sudden flight,
> but they, while their companions slept,
> were toiling upward in the night.
> Then, she would close with:
> Mom loves you.

Why San should feel the need to continue this trend into their adult life is a question that could be debated ad infinitum. Deep down, human beings, no matter how old, want to experience loving care. We live for that personal touch.

San's kitchen transforms into her creative space while making breakfast for her girls. Crayola crayons sit beside scissors, glue and blank Post-It notes on which she will create beautiful and inspiring works of art she will stick to their lunchboxes.

It is through these rituals they learn to take care of self. This kind of communion helps them to bond and peer pressure becomes less threatening. They are eating mindfully and over time this practice becomes perfected. It is all about balance and developing the confidence that is transferrable to other areas of their lives. Body and mind in harmony.

Writing love-notes to your children may make you feel vulnerable, awkward and sappy at times but it is the best thing you can do for yourself and your children. Love letters put smiles on people's faces. Some people treasure these gems. A teaspoon of love sprinkled over hearty meals is nutrients for the brain, the command center of the human body, which guides every intelligent operation we need to survive, grow and make sense of the world.

Writing love letters is not reserved for the hopeless romantic. *The Bible* abounds with love letters King Solomon wrote to his son David. Critically acclaimed writers like F. Scott Fitzgerald, while penning some of the most memorable narratives like *The Great Gatsby*, took quality time to write loving letters to his daughter. The act of writing thoughtful letters to someone who is sick or lovesick can be therapeutic.

David Epston and Michael White have conducted groundbreaking research in the power of story to heal. Their practice, called *Narrative Therapies*, is now widely accepted throughout the world. The therapists have employed storytelling orally and in the form of the written word to shift the perspective of the sufferers from helpless victim to persons in control of their lives. In some cases the change is stunning. Here for example is David Epston writing encouragingly to an anorexia patient:

> "I strongly felt Anorexia, once again, pulling you away from us and down, insinuating that there was no other 'world' for you other than his hell, where you might sit beside him as his Queen. I am writing to you in defiance of Anorexia and all that it stands for. I swear to you – and all those murdered by Anorexia are my witnesses – that

nothing will prevent the League from keeping a 'place open for you – a place to stand and take a stand for your life and entitlements to happiness, peace and fulfilment ..."

One might think the letter dramatic but then so is the real life battle of the person who is anorexic. Over the years, this type of therapy has gained respect. The act of writing the letters takes the feelings and attitudes out of the subconscious and exteriorizes them, giving them physical substance. These patients or clients were better able to see their situation.

Now here was San doing the same thing thousands of miles away with no knowledge of David Epston and Michael White. Even though her letters are of a different length, they are helping to create a reality of love – another way of giving love physicality. She benefits from the exercise as well. "When I write my love letters to my children in the mornings, I am at peace when I leave home for the 30-mile commute on the highways. I never had road rage, and within an hour, I meet my clients with kindness. Letter writing sends a different energy to my psyche."

A little San love is a good idea. How about sending a love-note to your son or daughter who is away serving in the military for his or her country? Your letter could be the calm they need to balance unrest. Talk with your children – you will be amazed how much they are growing as thinkers with strong morals right before your very eyes. If we model this kind of sensitivity they will model it for their children and those who fall within their sphere of influence later in life. Children, who are fed thoughtful words, develop emotional health, a key quality for success.

Affirmation: *I am grateful to see the connection between the body and the mind. I love and nurture both body and mind. I am well. My children are well.*

Chapter 20

Quantum Action

March on, and fear not the thorns, or the sharp stones on life's path.

—Khalil Gibran

My job is too demanding. Everything that needs to be done properly, I have to do it myself. From taking a simple telephone message to writing a memo that communicates time-sensitive messages to the staff. Nobody will hire someone in their fifties. That's too much on a company's budget. I am literally falling apart.

These woeful mantras make their way to our dining tables, our bedrooms, our places of worship, the gym, among our friends. So many of these are the voices of parents desperately in need of a new career but feel paralyzed to forge new territory. What's holding us captive to the jobs we don't enjoy? Getting a pension from our first and only job is no longer the norm? That trend changed significantly in the 1990s. Every day, our body has to restore with new cells to keep us going. It means we are naturally predisposed to change. Yet, we are afraid to take risks. Sometimes we get stuck in positions where there is no challenge, no intellectual stimulation and no growth. The shipwreck feels safer than a fresh start. Newton's first law of motion says "Every object persists in its state of rest ... unless it is compelled to change that state by forces impressed upon it." This is natural law working in our world and working in our lives.

In simple terms, if you have to take action and put in motion what you desire to happen in a given time, you have to be compelled to change and not from the outside but from within yourself. Is your desire strong enough? You don't have to have all the answers. You just have to have the desire and take action. And sometimes that action must be as big as your desire.

Take the story of mountaineer Aron Ralston who was hiking alone in the Canyonlands National Park and got trapped by a falling boulder. The news reports that after the sixth day with no hope of food or rescue, he made the decision to break his arm and saw himself free.

His story made international news in 2003. Aron could have accepted death. He chose life and was unwavering in his resolve. Here is what Anthony Robbins calls "massive and determined action" at work to survive and fulfill one's purpose in life. To use Newton's words, there was a part of Aron that "compelled" action after being a close companion with death for five days. So strong was his desire, his resolve, that he had the strength to climb out of a narrow canyon, rappel himself down another sheer canyon wall with one arm and walk to the help (a family on vacation) waiting for him.

Author and academic Ralston "Rex" Nettleford grew up in abject poverty in rural western Jamaica. He studied by lamplight and walked barefooted long distance to school, rain or shine. Rex had a vision for his life and knew that education would be his ticket out of poverty. At twenty four, he won the prestigious Rhodes Scholarship and would later become an advisor to Prime Ministers and other heads of government in the Caribbean region. He was a master at timing. In 1962, the very year Jamaica gained its independence from Britain, Rex and his friend Eddie Thomas formed the internationally acclaimed *National Dance Theatre Company of Jamaica*. Rex could have let the walk to school deter him. The dirt roads were hot and filled with sharp stones and they were long. Newton's third law is at play here. "For every action there is an equal and opposite reaction." This third law is implied in flight. Nettleford's strong desire made him walk to school, and walking to school sustained his desire for education. With help from two powerful women in his childhood who recognized his abilities, he rose from the ashes of scarcity to the heights of academic, political, artistic and cultural power.

Nelson Mandela survived twenty-seven years in prison, some of those in solitary confinement in Apartheid South Africa. Yet he became the president of South Africa and won the Nobel Peace Prize. Winnie Mandela and the anti-Apartheid system kept his name alive, but he could easily have succumbed and be a martyr for the cause while in prison. Instead, his quantum action was to prepare for his long delicate "war of attrition" fought without bullets. Elie Wiesel survived the horror of the German death camps in World War II to become a Nobel Laureate, a published author, professor and more importantly, a human rights advocate and campaigner against genocide around the world. Quantum action may be psychological – a digging deep to find out what you are made of, the will to survive in spite of overwhelmingly "negative" circumstances.

In the African country of Malawi, the courageous campaign by teen, Memory Banda, raised the legal marriage age to eighteen years old. Prior to March of 2015, the practice for eons was to initiate girls as early as pre-pubescent girls in preparation for marriage. Despite ridicule in her community, Memory refused the destructive practice at fifteen years old. Her younger sister, Mercy, was not so lucky and was sent to be 'sexually cleansed' at the initiation camp at eleven years old. She became pregnant and was forced to marry.

By the time Mercy was sixteen, she was twice divorced with 3 children. She's lucky as some child brides die before that age. Imagine what it takes to change a country and a deeply held cultural norm. Memory's quantum action was to join with Malawi NGO group *Girls Empowerment Network*, become an advocate and take the matter to the Malawi Parliament. Memory's action has changed the future for Malawi women.

If you really want to make a change in your life, brainstorm and find out what sets you on fire. What is it your heart's desire and are you doing something every day to make that desire a reality? Now some of us already know what needs to be done but we don't have the will to do it. It simply means more effort. Study the masters. Take a Tony Robbins, Deepak Chopra or Les Brown on-line seminar or read one of their books. These guys are life hackers and have mastered the art of motivating themselves. Robbins and Brown have beaten the odds. They were poor at one time with no conscious blueprint of how to change their circumstances. Still they dug deep, responded when the universe called. In Robbins words, they took "massive and determined action."

If there is no action, there is inertia and you don't get the response from life that you desire. This physical law governs everything.

Affirmation: *I know that I must make a significant change in my life. Therefore, I take conscious action to get rid of stumbling blocks. My actions speak louder than my problems.*

Chapter 21

Nature's Season

To everything there is a season, and a time to every purpose under the heaven.

—King Solomon

Seasons are a vital expression of life on the planet. There is the new birth of spring and the transitional nature of fall. Summer is loud with passion and winter goes within. In tropical climates where there are not many seasons, Nature defines them as dry and wet season. Even the desert has its ranges of expression, its ups and downs. We should take some pointers from Nature and from the people who understand its rhythms, to plan the seasons in our lives.

Farmers are in touch with Nature's signals. From time immemorial, farmers have been preparing for the effect the winter freeze has on crops and animals and so they must prepare way ahead of time. Since the 18th Century, the *Farmer's Almanac* has been a bible for those whose lives and livelihood depend on the weather. Farmers seek shelter for their livestock. They pickle the vegetables, make bacon, freeze fruits and chop enough firewood for the long haul.

Education has its own seasons. No different than the *Farmer's Almanac* is the Department of Education's *College Preparation Checklist* guiding the parent and student towards the many milestones from as early as middle school. Parents know when to start researching and applying for financial aid for the college bound.

The summer holiday are built for outdoor fun. So we begin early in the year to look for summer programs. In my family, it is dance camp for my granddaughter, the gym for her mommy and professional development workshops and writers conferences for me. During the fall and winter, children need warmer wardrobes. Many of us stock up on vitamins, cold and flu medicines. Then there are the various religious holidays. Those of us who are strapped for cash do what we can to rise to the occasion. We clip coupons. Though Thanksgiving is a holiday with deep meaning, Black Friday sales are now part of the ritual, an opportunity for people to stow away their upcoming Christmas gifts.

Have you ever noticed that every year without fail, certain events occur in your life? You can set your calendar by these cycles. I call these personal seasons. August and September happen to be renewal months for me. I get a surge of energy and an almost superhuman ability to maintain my focus for long periods. I get a lot of creative work done. If I am changing my job, invariably that key decision was made in October and November. The same phenomenon occurs when I need to break away from social or professional groups, no longer in harmony with my goals. For me it's a time of transition. I have to watch my finances in spring. If I don't, my summer will be a major financial downturn. We need to know these personal seasons so we can anticipate and prepare for them.

Then there are the emotional seasons. We have no control over the cause but how we respond to that season is key to progress. It was going to be our first winter without our mother. We had spent the entire summer with her hospice care and then the inevitable happened: she transitioned. We had done everything we could in preparation for this chilling loss; well so it seemed. But the winter came and Mama was no longer with us. For me, things started to fall apart at work and I had no strength to bear it. Every little situation became monumental. It would take the entire winter for me to go inward and seek the help I needed to cope with this profound loss. I started to meditate, exercise more, read the experts on grief and journal. I even watched Oprah Winfrey's inspiring *Super Soul Sunday*.

This emotional winter changed the trajectory of my life. My future became crystallized. I began speaking at parent seminars, developing virtual curricula, writing and co-producing a high school musical. Meanwhile, this book and others were conceived. That's what winter did for me when I went inward. I do not want to mislead you that everything is perfect but what I do know is that everything is in Divine order. This emotional winter was the season for stillness and recalibration.

Stress will have parents running on empty from one season to the next. We can lower our stress and recalibrate, plan ahead more carefully and strategically for our personal wellbeing. If we do not become strategic, we violate that air pilot's inflight oxygen rule to take care of ourselves so we can take care of others. Take stock of yourself. Evaluate things you could have done better and things you did well. Some folks experience great sadness even depression during the winter because the days are shorter. This could be an opportunity to go to your doctor and get much needed vitamins and minerals to boost your immune system and work on your coping skills. If you can meditate, do short twenty minute or ten minute sessions in the morning and before bedtime. You can play with the frequency and duration. Some people have been known to take a bathroom break and do a five minute meditation session.

Look to the wisdom of Nature and the Divine manifesting in the physical seasons in order to master our lives. Our personal seasons are vital too. There is a time for us to be quiet and inward focusing and there is a time for us to be social. There is a time for us to be strategic planners and clear the clutter. Going against the tide causes undue stress. Let us prepare like the swallow for migration or squirrel by putting away our nuts and fruits for the winter. This way, we adapt to environment so we can rest, restore and balance life for ourselves and our children.

Affirmation: *This work that I do is purposeful and carefully planned in its season. I reap the mature fruits of my labor, abundantly. I am energized and revitalized every day. My children are energized and revitalized every day.*

Chapter 22

Critical Thinking

Children see magic because they look for it

—Christopher Moore

As if in approval of my journey, the digital sign displayed 'Good Service' for the express train to Grand Central Terminal. This was not the morning to hurry. I was on my way to speak to a gathering of parents on *Common Core State Standards*. I would be placing tools directly in parents' hands for them to better partner with the teacher to nurture successful children and inspire the magic of learning.

I continued to mentally prepare for my presentation and Q&A. What do I do if parents respond to my take on the common core as if it was a horror movie, *A Nightmare on Elm Street*? The train horn hooted. Metro North was on time. The conductor held my hand and guided me onto the full train. A boy of 4, I later learned his age, was kneeling on a three-passenger seat, looking out the window while his dad sat facing him on the opposite seat. I took a seat next to the boy. I closed my eyes to center myself but I was drawn to the curious boy's rapid questions which he hurled at his father. The conductor announced: This is Harlem. One hundred and twenty-fifth street. The boy echoed without a hitch: "One hundred and twenty-fifth street. Daddy, look. The Statue of Liberty!"

"No, we are only in Harlem. The statue is closer to Grand Central, near to my office."

"No, it's the statue."

The boy was right. There was a poster on the billboard at the station inviting visitors to see Lady Liberty in the harbor. At that point, I entered the conversation confirming that the boy had indeed observed a picture of the Statue of Liberty. He continued hurling questions. Clearly, his expectations of his father's knowledge of all things ranked high in his world. He sat still for a while and then exclaimed, "Why is the train going backwards, Dad?"

"The train is not going backwards, son."

"Yes it is. It is going backwards." Not satisfied with his dad's response, he folds his arms and studied the motion of the train moving steadily along the tracks. Then suddenly, the youngster had an epiphany. "O my back is turned to where you work! Right Dad? We are not going backwards then."

"We are going forward, son."

I had a topic and talk prepared but now felt I had to include this event in my presentation. I was being shown deductive reasoning at work in the mind of a four year old boy. His dad and I chatted for a good ten minutes about adolescent apathy and lack of curiosity. We reminisced about the good old days when information was not readily at our fingertips and we had to work and play with our siblings and friends to discover new things about the world – new things about ourselves. He confided that he wished his parents had spent more time with him during his high school years. Somehow, in our culture, the magic of curiosity has all but disappeared for adolescents. I shared that this is exactly what I hope to teach the parents in my presentation – inspiring the magic in adolescent thought.

How do we keep this young boy's enthusiasm going? By keeping communication open. Becoming engaged in his exploration. Don't be threatened by unusual behavior. He did something different and learnt some physics in the bargain. Dad was relaxed and so was he. Even a train ride is an opportunity to learn. However, stress and fear can get in the way of this communication. Some parents would most likely have told him to sit quietly. Watch out for accidents and use his inside voice.

We keep the young boy's curiosity going by first recharging our own curiosity no matter our age. Director and producer Brian Grazer says two vital things about curiosity. He describes it as "democratic" and available to all. In his book *A Curious Mind*, he tells the story of eavesdropping on a conversation outside his apartment window. As he listened, he got the lead on a job, made the call and landed the job at *Warner Brothers* the next day as a legal clerk. It was his intro into show business and he never looked back. Curiosity saved him and found him his life's mission. "As a boy, I peppered my mother and my grandmother with questions, some of which they could answer, some of which they couldn't. By the time I was a young man, curiosity was part of the way I approached the world every day... My kind of curiosity is a little wide-eyed, and sometimes a little mischievous. Many of the best things that have happened in my life are the result of curiosity."

As Grazer points out, curiosity can be suppressed, giving examples of political suppression. Stress can suppress our natural curiosity. If as adults and elders we allow our curiosity to be suppressed because of stress, pain and fear, then we don't hear the little boy or girl asking questions about life.

Something changes during adolescence we both agreed. Teens want their independence. Parents stop having fun learning with teens. Although these hormonal years sometimes come loaded with angst, it's not too late to try. Let's think of one fun thing we can learn along with our teenagers in the coming weeks. I agree with George Bernard Shaw who once said: "We don't stop playing because we grow old; we stop playing because we stop playing."

Affirmation: *I stay open to the magic of life. I can look at the world through the eyes of my child with honesty, freshness and flexibility. I remain open to the magic of learning.*

Chapter 23

Absence

Don't wait. The time will never be right.

–Mark Twain

Jordan was three when his father joined the United States Army. His recollection of his father was a man whose brown face was covered with curly black hair and a scary beard who threw him up in the air a lot. Even though he was a mere toddler he can remember the laughter and the pleasure as he flew through the air. For thirteen years, Jordan carried around that image in his head while he wondered why his father disappeared. He didn't ask his mom about his father anymore. But his gut quickened whenever he saw a bearded man looking like his dad on the street or in a crowd. He got an earful from his mom about his dad when he did something that displeased her. She would say: "You are just like your father. You cannot be depended on to do the right thing." He thought it was so unfair and it made him want to defend his dad even though he had abandoned them.

"Mom that's a generalization. This is just one incident!" he'd shout.

Seeing other dads cheering on their children at football and soccer games made him depressed. By the time he was sixteen years old, his best buddies had already spent a year in the Junior ROTC. Jordan's anxiety grew. His pals were doing the posting of the American flag at the annual school's graduation exercise or at special official assemblies. Jordan joined the JROTC in his sophomore year. He was feeling his dad's absence even more and was now looking for him online. There were so many men with that name. Why was he searching anyway? His dad didn't really want him or he would be at home.

Two years later, in his senior year, he was sitting on a bench in the courtyard waiting his turn to see the Army recruiters. Two recruiters walked by, one laughing as he told a story. The laugh was so familiar. As they disappeared through the doors his stomach fluttered. He swallowed repeatedly. The feeling of doom was so intense that he wondered if he should even bother signing up that day. Why was he feeling so ill? This was supposed to be the best day of his life. It wouldn't be cool to barf in front of these men. He loved the military.

    Finally, Jordan met with three young recruiters. He wiped his sweating face with the back of his hand as they shared the entire plan of training and services. They recommended he take home the application and discuss the matter with his family but Jordan didn't want to do that. His mom would have something negative to say about it. He continued flipping the pages. He hesitated briefly before completing the "father' slot on the form thinking bitterly that his father was missing out.

    Jordan was directed to hand over the completed packet to an older Army Officer who examined each page, carefully and meticulously. He wondered why the officer spent so much time with his paperwork considering the other students got processed more quickly. The officer finally growled that he would be back in a minute and disappeared in the direction of an office in the far corner. A minute turned into fifteen. Still feeling unsettled Jordan glanced at the clock on the wall. Three-thirty. He'd just go straight home instead of hanging out with his friends.

    The officer returned but sat there for a few minutes, shuffling the papers. "Maybe he doesn't want me in the army," Jordan thought. He was about to ask the recruiter to give him back his application and so he scanned his badge to address him respectfully by his name. Much to his surprise, both he and the Army Officer had the same first and last names. He felt as if he was floating and grabbed on to the desk for support. The man looked up from the papers and gazed in Jordan's eyes. It was the same man who had been laughing earlier. A glint of recognition flashed.

"No, this is not possible. This man is my dad. I just know it."

The beard was gone and he had a close shaven head and big bald spot. Something shifted in an even deeper place inside Jordan as they searched each other's eyes again. It was a longing they both felt over the years that had been realized in the most unlikely space – the space where Jordan often felt loneliest, at school, among his friends. The officer cleared his throat and half coughed. Jordan knew he was feeling the same thing too.

"Come this way and close the door behind you." He gestured with his hand toward the office.

Shell-shocked, Jordan did as he was told. His dad flipped the "Do Not Disturb" sign on the door then closed it. In the privacy of the office, Jordan and Army

Officer Jordan Theodore Bankhead sat for a while, Jordan's heart drummed hard as if he was on one of his training runs. At first, they spoke in fits and starts with long silences between them. Jordan worried that his silence would drive the man away. He just didn't know what to say and his tongue felt heavy as he formed his words. Then the floodgates opened and Jordan plied the officer with questions. His dad had come back to the area only six months ago from San Francisco. Several times the impulse came to ask his dad why he had left but he squashed it. He wanted most to be in the room with him. He felt a little afraid that this was a dream. He didn't want to wake up.

"Mom said I was just like you. I guess she was right." Jordan joked and didn't feel embarrassed to be laughing and crying.

At 17:30 they shook hands, then gripped each other. Even though they promised to meet later, Jordan left reluctantly, feeling that slight fear in the pit of his stomach. His head reeled when he imagined what his mom would say when she came home. He decided then and there he would go to her workplace instead. He dialed her cell phone number.

"Mom, I'm coming to meet you."

What is the likelihood that Jordan would be standing face to face with his own father at the army recruitment table? For years, his longing for his father drew him to everything army: movies like *Saving Private Ryan, Pearl Harbor, The Last Samurai* were among his favorite war stories. Jordan often felt that he was not hearing the entire story – his father's story was missing. He was right. It's human for children to want to know both parents. Keeping secrets creates fragility. We can see from the story that Jordan, though he may appear to have a healthy relationship with his mother, still has some fear of rejection, depression and loneliness. Research is showing that whether the parent's absence is due to divorce, military action, death, or incarceration, or absence from birth, the child suffers from the absence of connection.

As a parent, there were times when I could have used a shoulder to cry on, some reassurances that I was doing the right thing by my daughter. Some parents need a toolkit to help their school age children through the awkward years? Even though she had strong study habits, I needed to have the right answer to the question, "Mom, why isn't Dad here anymore?" I cried when I thought I had privacy but unbeknownst to me, my daughter could see it. I smiled a lot when I was confronted but I didn't fool her one bit. My responses gnawed at her in the most inopportune times. It's going to pop into her consciousness in class during the day.

For a very long period of time, she worried about me and grew angry at her dad. At ten years old she challenged me and told me "You lied to me." She was right. I did so by omission in an attempt to spare her pain. It was clear then that I had added to her stress, that I had caused her pain anyway. Research now shows that stress affects memory, recall and the ability to focus. Students need large doses of these in school to do well. Don't put a Band-Aid on the problem. I did not have to tell her the entire story but I owed what was necessary and kind.

Not all problems can be blamed on parents. Children have come from seemingly well balanced two-parent homes and still turned out to be sociopaths. Not all fatherless children become statistics. In 2013, two education experts appeared on the *Oprah Life Class* to help advance the discussion on absent fathers in America. Geoffrey Canada and Dr. Steve Perry, both very successful in advocacy had come from homes without fathers. A child can lose a lot when Dad is missing from the home.

Though TV talk shows are not always dependable sources of in-depth information on certain topics, this particular *Life Class* was revealing. It was the first time, the camera in a very deliberate way, had exposed to millions some of the pain that men were feeling about this topic. There wasn't a dry eye among the men at the conference. Why was there so much pain and tears? After all, men generally present a stiff upper lip, stoic when it comes to showing sensitivity.

When asked for the definition of fatherhood, Canada who is the creator of the *Harlem Children Zone*, said,

> "I really believe there is a male energy in Life that is part of being a whole and I just find that kids need the person whose first tendency is to lift them up off their feet, to roll around with them, to throw them high enough ... that sense of the yin and the yang ... helps to make us whole people and we are constantly reaching out for that other part of ourselves that's missing... And you can actually feel that energy in my opinion and I think that part of a father's role. His role is to be this kind, loving disciplinarian ..."

In fact Dr. Steve Perry said in all his life, he'd never purchased a father's day card. These two experts prove that moms are rearing successful boys despite the statistics saying otherwise.

Geoffrey Canada's comment on fatherhood reminds us about an important fragment of memory Jordan had. Jordan was a young child when his father left but he too remembers the feeling of his father throwing him in the air introducing him to key qualities of fearlessness, fun and self-control. According to a 2006 study, *The Importance of Fathers in the Healthy Development of Children* by Jeffrey Rosenberg, "fathers' play has a unique role in the child's development, teaching, for example, how to explore the world and how to keep aggressive impulses in check." This child play between Jordan and his dad could account for him not being an aggressive teen. But that is not the only experience defining happiness and success. Jordan has felt depressed, a problem facing many teens in today's society. Depression when not managed prevents healthy social interaction and threatens self-confidence.

It is so important to explain the absent parent to our children. It's the elephant in the room. Wishing and praying that problems will not appear is not enough. When children ask, find loving and necessary ways to tell them the truth and complete the gap. Of course, this is a grey area. Not all truths are necessary especially for little children who are developing. For example, if a parent's absence means rejection, then the parent in the home has to be prudent. As parents, we can't tell the child he or she is unwanted. Instead, we are obligated to tell a gentler and emotionally supportive story about Dad's absence and fill in for him by teaching those principles that Dad would teach.

Abandonment and rejection can leave a stain on a child's identity. He or she can carry this stain into adulthood. Bob Marley says it best: "Tell the children the truth." Truth changes attitude and builds resilience.

Affirmation: *I will first be honest to myself and then to my children. Because I love my children, I am duty bound to honor their full heritage. It is my duty to honor their feelings. I speak this truthfully.*

Chapter 24

Bust on the Bully

If you know the enemy and know yourself, you need not fear the results of a hundred battles.

–Sun Tzu

All six feet three inches of his wide shoulders, ripped muscles tensely focused on the ball for a few seconds as it sails downfield. Then he joins the play, following the trajectory of the ball. Seeing an opposing midfielder setting up to receive the ball on a dribble, Kirk charged the player. When the dust cleared the opposing player had to be removed from the game on a stretcher and Kirk earned the yellow card. This would not be Kirk's last foul. He was ejected from the match.

The coach had talked to Kirk about his behavior on the field but not wanting the boy to lose too much of his edge, he'd refrained from taking any disciplinary action. But those moments on the field when the boy had been carded looked like aggression, not accidents in the line of play. The coach wondered what was causing his change in behavior. Asking the young man if he needed help had not worked. If something wasn't done soon, the boy wouldn't have a future in soccer. He set up an intervention with Kirk's parents and the school counselor to find a solution. He couldn't be worried about any feeling of betrayal. Save the team. Save Kirk.

From the start, Coach could see that all was not well with the family. Kirk greeted the adults politely when he entered the room. Kirk's mom, a tall regal woman rubs his shoulder in return. Kirk's father does not acknowledge him. There is an awkward silence. The guidance counselor kicks off the conversation. "Do you know why you are here, Kirk?"

"Yes. To be tortured!" Kirk responded with a slight smile.

Coach Granby, toggling a soccer ball from one hand to the other, took a step forward and looked Kirk dead in the eyes: "No, you are here to save your athletic scholarship. Don't throw away a great opportunity."

"Coach is right, Kirk," his mother added. "You know better. Can you tell us what's going on?"

"Hush your mouth Jean!" The father exclaimed.

He turned swiftly to the boy. "You are a nobody."

"How could you say such a thing? He made the team. He is our son for crying out loud."

"No. He's your son. You never let me discipline him like a man should a son."

"That's because you spend way too much time trying to discipline me as if I am the child."

"I don't have time to waste. Let's get on with this meeting. I am sure Coach Granby and the good counselor here has other pressing matters other than the jock and his mother's drama."

"This is the pressing matter! You were never available to come to his games. Why are you here anyway?"

"To see how I can save my pension money."

"Mr. and Mrs. Wilmot, this is neither the time nor the place for this. We need to come up with a plan that supports Kirk considering he has been exhibiting a lack of emotional fitness and team spirit."

"I could have told you Coach. They are a bunch of hypocrites," Kirk shouted and rushed towards the door.

Kirk's father was at the door before he got there, Kirk's jersey bunched up in the older man's right hand. His left was raised to strike. There was thick silence in the room. It was clear that the man had done this often. His wife was sitting with her head down. Kirk was trembling. There was no sign of his usual aggression on the field.

"Sir. You can't do that here," the Guidance Counselor insisted in almost hushed tone as she tried to retrieve the papers that fell on the floor.

The coach had seen enough. This problem wouldn't be easily solved from inside the home. He tried to ease the tension.

"Sir. It's okay. Everything is calm here." Kirk's father released him and went back to his chair.

From a safe distance, Kirk cleared his throat again and again to clear what suspiciously sounded like tears. He muttered under his breath. "They hate me. You think I don't come to school for a better life?"

The older man turned beet red. He looked ready to grab Kirk again. The coach held Kirk's eyes for a while, signaling him to be silent. It didn't work so he spoke more firmly.

"Young man, we need your full cooperation. If you do not make a change in your attitude in the next ten days, you will be expelled from the team. Is it worth it to risk losing your athletic scholarships? You have a responsibility to yourself and the team. It is all in your hands."

"I hear you, sir."

Following the intervention, his coach introduced him to the art of meditation. In the first three days, he was skeptical and resistant but felt deep inside that he wanted to win this one – he wanted to realize his dreams of becoming a soccer player like his idol, Pele. Meditation helped him become aware of himself and the number of times that he got angry. It gave him the ability to think or breathe before action. Later, it afforded him clarity of vision and was helping him to set realistic goals for himself and his team. In the second semester before graduation, Kirk built up the courage to apologize to his team. They kidded with him and slapped him on the back and a few of them assumed the pose. All was forgiven.

Thankfully, the practice of meditation has been gaining ground here in the west. As people face a stressful environment, they are turning to natural means to bring their life in balance. Hugh Jackman who plays the Wolverine character in *X-Men* talks about the effects of meditation on his life.

"Through meditation on a daily basis, I get to strip away the masks that we build—that I build for myself, small and large—to reach more of a feeling of my true self: Oh, this is who I really am. This is how I can experience life. Oh, I see. It's just something simpler, finer and more powerful ... I sense there has been a change, but the change brought me back more to my true nature as opposed to an acquired nature."

Jackman says his anxiety level dropped tremendously when he meditated. Others have found that too.

George Lucas is a long time meditator and is rumored to have gotten his inspiration for *Star Wars* during his meditations. Rock star Sting is also a famous meditator. Experts recommend you plan to sit for 15-20 minutes per day to meditate. Those who find it difficult can pare it down to 10 minutes a day early morning or before bedtime. Although the goal is to still the mind, start where you are. Following the sound and feel of the breath is the easiest way to start the practice. A little goes a long way.

Toxic relations with spouse and partners can have irreparable emotional and social damage to a child. Some children may function well in society beyond this experience and others will not. Talk to your children about your expectations for all of you. Start loving yourself out of a bad situation. Kirk's healing was so significant that he was able to write about it in his Statement of Purpose Essay for college: "We may not be able to change what happens around us but we can change what happens inside of us."

Affirmation: *My children are here to be loved and nurtured so they can grow into their best selves. They are not here to protect me from myself and those I allow to hurt me. I am a mirror for the way they learn resilience and love and I find healthy ways to help them learn these principles.*

Chapter 25

Ask Questions

Don't just teach your children to read; teach them to question what they read. Teach them to question everything.

–George Carlin

As a child, I was a serious questioner. Needless to say, I got into trouble on many occasions when I challenged adults, including my teachers, about cultural norms and belief systems. Some things just did not add up and I would relentlessly go in search of answers, much to the displeasure of some elders. Getting cautioned with "curiosity kills the cat," could have been a deterrent. The cross-eyed adult stare could have cut away at my self-confidence but my desire to know was stronger. I read everything I could wrap my often sweaty palms around and I could talk to my dad about what I read. He was a rare breed in my community. So I fared better than some of my peers.

As a teacher, I entered the high school classroom determined to do my share to help stamp out that attitude. In the classroom, I knew the trend hadn't changed. Over time, I realized some students were way too reserved or vulnerable to be caught asking questions. Some thought questioning is a sign of ignorance, a sign that the questioner doesn't know enough and not a sign that the questioner wants to know more. There is a subtle difference. That seed has to be planted early. I believe that the home is where we have the opportunity to teach children the difference between these two attitudes.

Jasmine Lawrence was first introduced to the world on the *Oprah Winfrey Show*. Five years earlier, she entered a contest for young entrepreneurs but she did not win. She continued to live the life of a typical young girl when the unthinkable happened. Jasmine was at the vulnerable age of eleven when she lost her beautiful hair to a bad perm that left her with unsightly bald spots. As parents, we know that body image is the center of a young person's universe. But Jasmine didn't buckle under this horrifying incident. She began to ask deep questions about 'why' her hair fell out and 'how' she could prevent it from happening again. She wanted to prevent others from suffering a similar fate. Her research would lead her to natural products and to her establishing, *Eden Body Works*, a million dollar enterprise. Alchemy at its best. This shifted the course of her life. Despite her teenage success, she did not drop out of school; instead, she continued to explore the wonders of the world of robotics, her first love. Today, her platform as a motivational speaker answers many "How" questions.

    I often say to my students: what differentiates you from Einstein, Steve Jobs, LeBron James, P. Diddy, Lewis Latimer are the "Why" and the "How" questions that lead to the advancement of world culture in science, technology, the arts and sports. My students can never imagine a world without the iPhone or iTunes because Steve Jobs asked the how and why questions and came up with solutions. Students should make the best of every opportunity they get during class to create high level questions that require solutions. What students discover is that there is a lot they need to learn and the answers are accessible if they start with the question. Critical thinking helps children to look beyond the written page in order to solve everyday problems.

If questioning is such an important activity "why is it not a more common practice in science education?" This is Robert Vale's question on one of the problems plaguing scientific investigation in schools. He mentions some possible answers. The teacher is viewed as God but isn't. That cultural view prevents learners from asking difficult questions that may not have an immediate answer. His solution: A teacher should feel completely comfortable saying, "I do not know the answer to that question, but let me look it up—or let's look it up together." Many questions do not have quick, easy answers and thus become seeds for investigation. Students also should be able to teach their peers when they look up an answer to a question. In this model, teachers and students become partners in their mutual education.

His second discovery is that questioning is a skill and needs to be taught. Vale tells the story of watching Tibetan Buddhist monks learning to debate. It's a daily ritual which has -

> "One monk continually questioning another monk for an hour, often on esoteric points of Buddhist thought. The impressive aspect of this practice is how the monks use this method of questioning/answering to hone their skills in

logic and to probe complex questions. The questioning involves great mental concentration and intense exchange, punctuated by episodes of laughter and joy."

We need to transform our classrooms into these monasteries of inquiry and spirited discussions all aimed at stimulating the curiosity of our children. As a teacher I welcome this kind of creativity and collaboration.

How can parents facilitate this kind of questioning? It starts right there in the home and I believe it's the later years that are minefield. We know the early years are okay. We give the babies mobiles with colors, movement and sound to get their senses going. We give them tons of engaging toys. We teach them language. We encourage walking. A big shift happens after the child gains language. But add to that our hard work, worry and fatigue. Under those circumstances, we can easily dismiss the child who asks too many questions. Where is the line when a four year old child asks a long chain of whys before bedtime? I have had those moments. Breathe deeply before frustration burns your ears and try to resist the *because-I-said-so* response. Tell our young explorer you can discover the answers together at a designated time.

At certain ages even mealtimes encourage curiosity. You just might encourage the creation of a Lego meal or carrot dinosaurs. That's material science and art in action. As they grow older the methods change and so do the object of curiosity and as parents and teachers we have to keep in step. Simply volunteering how you spent your day and solved a problem is seeding the curiosity culture in your home. Start a conversation by telling them what problem you solved today, and then asking them the open-ended How did you solve your problem today? Or: How was your day as wonderful as mine? These questions can present an opportunity for thinking strategically and defining values. It doesn't matter if the problem is calculus, geography, current affairs, medical ethics, farming, crime or play time. Put it all on the table.

In some cultures children are not allowed to ask the "why" and "how" questions. It could be considered a sign of disrespect. As a result, these children straddling the cultures find themselves too paralyzed to speak up in class. It stymies their intellectual growth. We have to remember that children are little people with amazing minds. The story goes that Einstein, when his sister was born, thought she was a toy and asked where the wheels were. It's a valid question. We can only hope that his parents laughed, told him no and gave him a few comparisons to go on. The curious mind is first developed at home.

Affirmation: *I create a safe space for my children to question life so we all can grow into the persons we are meant to be.*

Chapter 26

Empathy

Love and compassion are necessities, not luxuries. Without them humanity cannot survive.

–Dalai Lama

The day Suzie gave birth to her litter of eleven puppies; I had mixed feelings. I was sad because my parents warned me never to go near Suzie because she needs space to protect her newborn puppies. She was so tired after birthing her pups that I was sure she could do with a big hug from me. In my childlike mind, Suzie had no reason to be mad when I approached the opening of the cellar to peep at her litter: red-brown, light-brown, two white like her and one gray. They came in an array of shiny coats and squinted eyes wincing and wiggling on her milk-swollen teats. When she growled every hair on my head stood on edge.

Some days I watched as Suzie bathed her puppies one-by-one with her wet tongue and pulled them close to her tender breasts. I would lay flat on my stomach outside the cellar listening to her puppies feed—it was like music. Suzie would take her paw and push aside a greedy puppy that was spending way too much time feeding with little care for its siblings. She was teaching her youngster to share. When they were strong enough to play, Suzie would call them together with her wagging tail and run around the yard. I remember one day a sudden downpour of rain called for quick rescue of the gray pup that could not move as swiftly as the others. Suzie picked the puppy up in her mouth and rushed it to safety. As the pups became stronger, I soon eased my way into their play.

One fateful Sunday evening, Mama decided to give away two of the puppies to her friend in the choir. Mama picked up two of the pups and put them in a box. Suzie was furious, she growled fiercely at mama. I thought she would bite Mama but Suzie withdrew and covered the rest of her litter. She used every muscle in her body to protect them. I felt Suzie's heartbreak at the loss of her two puppies. Next thing I knew, Mama was making arrangements with Brother Mac to give away Suzie and the entire litter.

"Why not give away Jack, mama."

"Jack is a man-dog and he is not littering the yard with all these puppies. Somebody has to take care of them and it's not Jack."

"I will take care of them, Mama."

Back then, it wasn't the practice to neuter. One by one she gave the puppies away to the neighbors and anyone who wanted a pet. It was time to go to Dada. He didn't fail. One pup could stay if I took care of it. That was a no-brainer for me. I was signing up to learn some valuable lessons. The puppy had to be fed and kept warm. I had to bathe him. It was my responsibility to recognize the signs of distress or sickness and get him the help he needed. Dogs were not allowed in the house but I named the puppy Rover and made him the best bed on the back veranda. These were some of life's biggest moments for me.

Anyone who has had a child will remember when your baby first shared his or her bottle and you fake nibbled and said thank you? You and baby went through a long period of sharing everything, toys, wet noodles, bits of chewed cookies. How they took pleasure in reaching out those gifts to you with their tiny hands. And did they not weep sometimes when your face showed sadness or fear. It could have been just them imitating their caregivers with no awareness of meaning or actual empathy. In *The Philosophical Baby*, psychologist and researcher Dr. Alison Gopnik argues for the latter.

> Newborns have never seen their own faces. To imitate facial expressions in particular, newborns must somehow map expressions to their feelings ... for babies imitation is both a symptom of innate empathy and a tool to extend and elaborate that empathy. Young babies know that Mom's joy or pain is the same as their own joy or pain.

These little souls are learning to give very early in life.

Even though we are hard-wired for empathy, parents still have to cultivate it in their children. Some of us have become desensitized by a culture that promotes radical individualism over emotional intelligence. We can always increase our capacity to understand another person's experience. Sometimes it takes a lifetime to learn that lesson. When we model a lack of empathy, there is a danger of the child showing a lack of feeling for his or her siblings, peers and pets.

Taking care of pets develop our capacity for empathy. But how about our neighbors who are going through a tough time; the homeless man at the corner;

Hurricane Katrina victims, an ill person on public transport? Statistically, every day of our life could yield an encounter with someone in need of help. This is where the tire hits the road. Some of us are able to shower our pets with love but it counts when we can display that same regard for humans.

Harriet Tubman's resistance against slavery and her empathy for those in the same position made her volunteer as the guide on the Underground Railroad to lead people to freedom. Despite the ever-present threat of discovery and death, she persisted. In moments of great human suffering, the heroes are the ones who go the extra mile even in the face of danger. Firefighters, Police Officers and EMTs are notoriously underpaid for the kind of work they do, yet they show up and it's not just because they are adrenaline junkies. They care.

As parents, we should be aware not just of the dangers around us. Whether the helping hand is planned or spontaneous, our children should witness us in action and we should explain to them why. It is an opportunity for them to see empathy in action and someone they love doing the job. Let them read stories of heroic figures taking action but let them see it in real time in their community. Help them recognize their empathy and feel okay with it when they give to the vulnerable, feed the less fortunate, or simply have a conversation with someone who is suffering. If possible, take them places. Travel to distant countries has a way of sloughing off xenophobia and opening the eyes and the heart.

Affirmation: *I feel empathy and I know it's safe. In this abundant place, I have enough to share: a kind word, a small meal, simple regard for my fellow human being who has a right to be here. I comfortably demonstrate empathy in front of my children. I show them that it's a natural part of who they are. We travel the world together knowing that sun shines on everyone.*

Chapter 27

Confidence

Dream no small dreams for they have no power to move the hearts of men.

—Goethe

The first evening Melrose walked into my adult literacy classroom, I perceived that she was someone special. She wore the biggest smile below her wide brimmed hat the tip of which touched her bifocal glasses. The sinewy lady placed her notebook and pencil on the desk, slung her pocketbook over the arm of the chair, grabbed the ends of her skirt with both hands and sat on the chair. At first, I could not tell her age but when it was her turn to introduce herself to the six students and me, I was floored. Melrose was eighty years old, a mother of ten children, and a grandmother of sixteen. The other students were in their thirties whose education was interrupted by the ups and downs of life.

Melrose was the exception to the rule. She had no formal education. All her knowledge was based on what she heard and lived. All her life she worked in the field like any man, plowing and planting to sell to the market. Melrose confides that she was abandoned. She was the eldest of seven children. Her parents and siblings went away to England and she was left behind with her grandmother. Melrose could not read. Although she could recite long passages from the Bible, she wanted to learn how to read them. She dreamed of being able to read the letters her favorite sister had been sending to her for nearly three decades.

"If I could read one letter I would be happy, miss. It's been too long."

"You will one day."

"Can you teach me to write her back?"

"I will."

Mind you, I was only sixteen years old and part of a government sponsored initiative to eradicate illiteracy in my community. My immediate approach was to center her lessons on her favorite Bible passage, "The Lord's Prayer." When I pointed out the words and pronounced them for the first time, her eyes sparkled like phosphorescent light bulbs. In only three lessons, Melrose could recognize repeated words. Her favorite word would be: forgive. This enthusiastic woman was reading at the first grade level in a year. Melrose could read road signs she grew up with but never knew the letters associated with each word. The day she was able read the headline that Queen Elizabeth II and her husband Prince Philip the Duke of Edinburgh arrived in her island home of Jamaica for a week-long visit, a whole new world opened up. A proud woman from day one, her self-esteem took a quantum leap.

Reading Advocate and published poet, Earl Mills read his first book at age 48. His turning point came when he was surprised by his pastor at short notice and asked to read a passage from the Bible. He stumbled through the passage and was embarrassingly exposed at the church meeting. He had excellent numeracy skills but he could not read. His more than 40 year-old secret was out. He sought help soon after that incident. In a very revealing interview with Rebecca Gross, he talked about the clever ways people hide the fact they can't read. "I'm in a rush" and "I don't have my glasses" are just the tip of the iceberg. Fear of being exposed kept him away from parent-teachers meetings and he couldn't help with homework. Mills had valuable advice

about fixing the most obvious weakness in literacy campaign in America. He pointed out that quite a few of the Ads targeting people who can't read are written Ads. If a person can't read, these Ads won't reach them. His solution:
> "I would say the voices of the people, the adults that have come forth and now have learned to read – [it would help] if people would tap into that resource. Because once you see someone that's your next-door neighbor, your co-worker, someone that you thought could read—when you see them achieve success, it makes you feel like if they did it, I can do it."

Shame is a complex mass of feelings, pain, actions and avoidances that weighs heavily on a person but thankfully, Earl Mills was able to unravel it. He knows the avoidances so well that can easily identify those who can't read. It's a helpful tool in his advocacy efforts.

This might not be your story, parents. Yet, it is the story of more than 30 million Americans who do not possess literacy and numeracy skills and young students are among this group. Most are parents who are not able to read well enough to write a letter to someone they love or read a poem or sacred text, or put their children to bed with a fairytale. It is never too late to help someone to fall in love with learning again. First, be observant and offer help with humility. As Earl Mills points out, there is a lot of shame and avoidance. If you know someone in this situation, offer inspiration by reading this and other success stories to that person. There is help at the local libraries. Some places of worship have programs for emergent readers. Children these days have access to so much information on the Internet.

Researchers have discovered that teaching what you learn, and as you acquire information, is one of the fastest ways to ground yourself in the knowledge. Teachers are always doing reading buddy exercises in their classes. The results of a 2004 study in which psychologist Elizabeth Meisinger observed elementary school children at work, added another layer of clarity to the approach. She and fellow researchers found that "providing basic partner reading script instruction at the beginning of the year was associated with better social cooperation during partner reading." Another of her recommendations was that "teachers ... allow children to choose their own partners." It is a confidence building tool. Her final caution: "pairings of low ability children with other low ability children and high ability children with other high ability children should be avoided."

What about early intervention? We can retrofit Meisinger's recommendations to the home environment.

It is going to be especially important for early detection of reading difficulties in our young children. Parents have been doing paired reading for eons. Sometimes as we read bedtime stories, our children also want to read and participate and sometimes we allow that. What we don't always do is keenly observe the reading play whether we have multiple children or a single child in the home. Because the home is more intimate, it's the perfect environment to try new approaches or try what the teacher does in paired reading in the bigger classroom setting. Confer with the teacher and find out what he or she recommends. In my view, Meisinger's findings let us know we can even switch reading roles. Let the child read a bedtime story to us on occasion.

Giving the gift of reading and writing to someone is a great way to build your service muscle and new readers well-being and quality of life. Melrose and Earl Mills found happiness because they asked for help, took action and banished the shame.

Affirmation: *When I open my mind to new knowledge my life expands and my children are enriched.*

Chapter 28

Self-Control

Midlife is the time to let go of a dominant ego and to contemplate the deeper significance of human existence.

–Carl Jung

We live and work in close confines with people whether in small or large homes, cubicles or corner offices. We rub shoulders with people on the train. Cars tailgate on the highway. For those of us with self-control, we avoid clashes. Our training, our disposition and our ability to control ourselves, help us recognize the traps as they are being made. We keep the ego in check and not let it lead. This way we consciously navigate through the day with our families, friends, coworkers and fellow students. This way we serve life.

There is an extremely disruptive kid I'll call Peter in my English Language Arts class. On the days when he's good he settles down and stays on task. He gets full marks on assignments. He works well with the team. He is a brilliant storyteller. This eleven year old instinctively knows the cardinal rules of storytelling. I don't have to drill them in his head. It's beautiful to watch him develop a theme and build a story around it. His stories have a beginning, middle and end and they are very engaging. On a bad day, Peter is out of control. He doesn't sit still in class and he doesn't complete assignments. He goes to all the other groups and starts a fuss and stays until he gets the last word. He's verbally abusive. He pulls on the girls' pigtails. His expletives often misogynistic. This is an out-of-control ego.

Though I am taking Carl Jung's quote out of context, we can't wait until midlife to help Peter. He needs an intervention and he needs it now. We understand children struggle during the puberty years but by eleven years old, Peter should have already developed some social skills. The boy has wreaked his brand of terrorism on more than one classroom. We follow the reporting protocol when he attacks his classmates yet they don't yield results. A few pre-suspension conferences with his parents and teachers have left us unable to solve the problem. Where is his rage coming from? Is it coming from the home environment? His parents say he doesn't behave in that manner at home. As teachers, we don't have the right to suggest that he needs to be tested but it may be time for a psychologist to enter into the picture. Issues of self-esteem may be the cause of Peter's outbursts and bullying in class.

Winning over the ego is an everyday task. One place the battle of egos plays out is on the crowded highway. Some drivers don't want others to get ahead of them so they step on the gas as the other driver tries to enter the flow of traffic. You the incoming driver had better carefully gauge your speed in this cat and mouse game. Nobody is exempt from the challenge of an out-of-control ego. In recent news, an Episcopalian priest was arrested on charges of aggravated assault in Florida for allegedly pointing a handgun at a driver who, he said, had been riding his bumper. Police found a handgun in his car.

The consequences of rage can be catastrophic. Some years ago a tragedy played out between Donald Bell and Timothy Mann in Sacramento. Donald Bell cut off Timothy Mann on the highway and it would later lead to a confrontation. Even though Mann's wife and son begged him to let it be, he confronted Donald Bell and punched him. News reports said Bell, who was angry, had his gun in plain view. Mann was too angry to fear the sight of the gun. When we are angry, we generally miss details we should see and hear. We could walk through fire. Bell fatally shot Mann in the face and he died on the spot. Bell's 15 year old son and Mann's son witnessed the traumatic incident. Two weeks later, Bell, probably now calm enough to consider that he'd snuffed out another life, went to the spot where he'd killed Timothy Mann and committed suicide.

The Ego wants to be first. It wants to be loved to the exclusion of everyone else. It feels fear and reacts to that fear. Jung says the Ego is only a small part of who we really are. There is constant communication between the Ego and the deepest part of ourselves. Confidence and high self-esteem are the result of listening to that deeper part of ourselves.

It is up to us to constantly monitor and listen to our deeper selves so we don't get into hand to hand combat with every person we meet. For me, simply taking a few deep breaths gives me the ability to take stock of the situation in a calm manner. I pass on that calm to others in my vicinity. It helps me to listen deeply and make better decisions.

The Peters of the world can't be told they are bad persons when they act up in class. In fact, Peter whose parents are educators is smart, verbose and aware of the constraints within which teachers work. He does not allow himself to be ejected from the classroom. So I hear him out. Knowing he needs attention I listen and he gets the last word.

Life teaches us through the effects of our actions that we can't allow the ego to get out of control. But some of us need special help to pay attention to and remember these moments. As a parent, get help from an expert. It does not mean you are labeling your child. It just means you are learning new ways to identify if you are, by your silence, enabling the behavior. Was there a loss in the home? Are Mom and Dad too busy? Dig into your Pandora's Box of memories to see if you suffered any of the same emotions as a child and now out of solidarity you go overboard, giving the child freedom to express his or her aggression. Become the friendly investigator and ask: Did I overdo it today?

Affirmation: *I am safe and I deserve to be loved. It's healthy to want the comforts of life. However, the ego is only a small part of who I really am. I am learning* *about who I really am. I breathe in. I listen. My children are safe and are learning how to give and receive love and respect. They are learning how to appropriately interact with all Life.*

Chapter 29

Goal Setting

It is the power of the mind to be unconquerable.

–Seneca

Their life on ice became the movie, Cool Runnings. Four men from a tropical island decided they wanted to master a sport that originated on the icy slopes in Albany, New York. Bobsledding. Anyone who knows Jamaica would think it absurd. There are no snow covered mountains in the Caribbean. In fact, visitors go to the Caribbean islands to escape winter. Yet, the possibility of conquering the ice has consumed Devon Harris and his team.

Few have electrified the world with their ability to dream other than their current reality. American boxer Muhammad Ali, a black man, refused to be defined purely by race. He mastered his sport, did his own publicity pre social media and changed the world.

Oprah Winfrey turned around the talk shows, the book industry and broke the stereotype of magazine cover models. Steve Jobs became obsessed about delivering beauty, functionality and technology in one package and had to keep trying till he got it right. African American Barack Obama became the first black US president and stayed in the White House for two full terms despite the sustained efforts of partisan politicians and the birther movement. We can learn from these individuals. They do not disappear at the first sign of trouble. They are remarkably persistent.

Harris did three Olympic tours: 1988, 1992 and 1998. Though his teams never medaled at these games, their post-game story is a winner. We study his example to gain more insight into the nature of goal-setting and persistence. Ben Franklin wrote in *Poor Richard's Almanack*: "Write injuries in dust, benefits in marble." Harris's attitude, his approach to life and his message to conference attendees and students are inscriptions on that marble.

As a young boy growing up in what had become one of Kingston's roughest areas, Harris dreamt big. He decided to change his attitude about the present and he refused to be hampered by a past where his parents struggled financially. He wanted to get out of poverty and avoid crime which was a natural next step for many young men in his hometown. To do this, he set goals and timelines and when he could, he changed his environment – the best high school led to the military where he could train, develop discipline and travel. Olympic Gardens, Jamaica and the Olympic Games, both hard places to live and win became proving grounds for Harris to do what Benjamin Franklin says, write your "injuries in the dust." With his inner mantra *Keep on Pushing* in his ear and heart he continues to define himself as Marley did before his death.

If ever there was a goal setting mantra, it would be that of the famous Bob Marley who once frequented another area of mine, Beechwood Avenue in Kingston where my aunt and cousins lived. Back then, the area wasn't as troubled as the Olympic Gardens of Harris's era but I recall Marley bopping through to sell his records. He had the 'rude-boy' trendsetter look and Rastafarian locks that were at the time a shock to the Jamaican psyche. Add to that his poor-man status. Things were stacked against him. In 1970, Marley released his song *Corner Stone*, a renunciation of the painful rejection he experienced at the hands of his father's family. The story goes, he approached them to get seed money to fund his music venture and was summarily dismissed as only some 'upper crust' will do. Apparently insulted but undeterred, Marley penned lyrics inspired by Psalm 118: 22: "The stone that the builders refused, is become the head stone of the corner" to rebuke the family. Against Jamaica's new rebel rhythm, the Biblical call-and-response song denounced this classicism plaguing the society at the time. The things people refuse are the things they should use followed with defiant cries of *Don't refuse me* and *Weep like a willow*. The song promised and Marley delivered. Bob Marley went on to put this unique music on the map which, 35 years after his death, is still topping the Billboard charts.

Life is a relay and how we pass the torch determines the success of the next runner, the next generation. Harris's children are benefiting from his change in attitude so many years ago. His children, especially his daughters have positive reinforcements. Often they see Dad leaving with his suitcase on the way to teach groups of people how to defy stereotypes. They are normal kids who want to watch TV on homework night and Mom has to negotiate with them to eat their veggies. When they fall down, they cry. Yet they are immersed in a success environment because they hear those encouraging words Dad says every day, *Keep On*

Pushing. Over time, those words will flourish in their consciousness. Calling them up will become as regular a habit as brushing teeth. The payoff is Ben Franklin's promise, our "benefit in marble." As parents, we need to create our success mantras like Harris and use them daily. The repeated mantra, the ability to see bigger than our current reality helps us to take action and, replace the defeatist inner programming currently inundating our daily lives.

Affirmation: *I can do anything. It's more than a buzzword. It's my prayer of agreement with the universe. I say it around the house so my children can hear it. I say it with emotion, with vigor, with gratitude, with laughter, through my tears, and I heal from the past. I mean it. My children are bathed in the emotion of it. I can do anything.*

Chapter 30

Sacred Space

Nothing has more strength than dire necessity.

–Euripides

The character James Bond had nothing over Ian Fleming his creator. A Jamaica Gleaner article says Fleming led a colorful life. He was a stockbroker turned spy in World War II and did some work for the CIA. The story goes he went to the exotic island of Jamaica for a naval conference and fell in love with the lush countryside of the northeast coast of Jamaica and promised to return "to write the spy novels to end all spy novels." He returned to the island, built a house called *Golden Eye*, and sent for his girlfriend British socialite, Lady Anne Rothermere. With the intention to leave Nature unspoiled, Fleming built a simple cozy house sitting fifteen acres of seaside land with a private white sand beach and crystal blue water.

The Flemings lived in Jamaica at least three months out of the year and *Golden Eye* became the birthplace of all thirteen of the James Bond's novels. His triangular writing table was made of rare exotic Blue Mahoe, the national tree of Jamaica. Per *Architectural Digest*, Fleming's working day began thus: "I wrote every one of the Bond thrillers here with the jalousies closed around me so that I would not be distracted by the birds and the flowers and the sunshine outside." Having lived in Jamaica, I know Fleming could not have shut out the sounds of the birds. Furthermore, the lushness of the surrounding would be branded on his consciousness. Even his bath and shower, in the open air surrounded by palm fronds were a nod to Nature. This was Ian Fleming's creative space, just the perfect amount of stimulation to bring in the muses.

Writers and artists in New York City know the value of sacred space but it often comes at exorbitant prices. As one who teaches during the day, I had to find a way to balance writing and teaching, two joys of my life. For one, I needed to dedicate time to write during the day especially in the early morning when the muses prefer to come looking for me. My muses don't wait for my summer vacation. My space, my *Golden Eye* was not going to be the lush private seaside spa resort in Oracabessa Jamaica. Something deep inside my gut told me that my *Golden Eye* was the New York City Lexington Avenue Express. I don't hear birds twittering in the background, just the clang, rumble and hoarse screams of metal on metal. The sounds do recede in the background when you get deep into a scene.

Trying to make teaching and writing work harmoniously was an imperative because I was beginning to put the writing on the back burner. On the other hand, I had way too many unfinished manuscripts. So, in September of 2013, with pen and journal in hand, I welcomed the muses and wrote for a precious 90 minutes on my way to school and the same 90 going back home. It was magical.

At the same time, I became immersed in Nature's richness, exotic peoples from around the world who use the train on a daily basis telling their stories in euphonic languages, the destitute poor shaking enamel pans soliciting coins punctuated by narratives so compelling about homelessness, hunger, their children lost in the foster care system, lack of health care – you could weep. Oh the telling sounds of New York City. As the train sped along miles of cacophonous clanging of railroad steel, through dark tunnels with an occasional flicker of light illuminating colorful graffiti, I wrote. Among other material, I was able to write the first draft of this book.

Maya Angelou rented a hotel room where she could write. Gertrude Stein would drive around and look at cows and write for 30 minutes per day. Chris Gardner, whose muses appeared in public bathrooms during a very challenging period in his life, inspired his award winning novel, *The Pursuit of Happyness*, which became a blockbuster film. Martin Luther King, Jr., wrote most of his books on the Caribbean island of Jamaica where he could feel a part of a culture where Blacks were a majority yet supported his dream of racial diversity? These writers would meet their muses in the most unlikely places of ritualistic worth – and the rest they say – is history.

We get our inspiration in the most unusual of places. For some folks the shower is the place for nirvana. Keep writing or recording on implements nearby or just keep running the scene or idea in your mind as the water runs. If quiet spaces inspire you, clean out that woodshed in your backyard and turn it into an outdoor spa or man cave. A friend of mine gets inspired walking through Ikea of all places. Your Lexington Avenue Express can be any vehicle. Sacred space is where you are. Under the stairs, on the train, in a closet, in the shower: sacred space is within.

Like us, sometimes our children fall in love with activities and places in which to enjoy them. For some, it might be finding that unusually quiet place in the house to train their imagination. I remember as a seven year old girl, regularly sliding under the bed to read. I would pull up a corner of the bed sheets and read my father's poetry book, the *Sonnets From The Portuguese by* Elizabeth Barrett Browning.

I dreamt about going places so I read Geography, of all topics, in this secret place. It was peaceful and away from my three interfering siblings. For some kids, it's the library on a weekend. Others, it is that corner in the classroom where the books on the shelves make them curious about other lands, peoples and cultures. Please allow them that sacred space. Check on them to make sure they are not doing anything dangerous but give them their creative space and the free playground of their imagination.

Affirmation: *Today, I recognize my sacred spaces and am grateful for the things that enrich my life and the life of my children.*

Chapter 31

Integrity

To conquer oneself is the best and noblest victory; to be vanquished by one's own nature is the worst and most ignoble defeat

–Plato

To the school community, Zeita and Ralph are model parents. They are undeniably the most involved parents in the lives of their three school-age children. Both parents attend every parent-teacher conference, swim meet, chess championship, little league football games and the fall and spring concerts in which their children actively participate. It is stressful to hear Zeita, the more competitive parent make demands of a coach, school teacher or administrator. She is ruthless in carving an advantageous spot for each child on the team by all available means – even if it means compromising the truth in front them.

Forever etched in my memory is the day I listened attentively to this mother of my 10 year old student concoct a story that her daughter completed and submitted her creative writing assignment. She accused me of misplacing the paper. The situation escalated. "You don't know my daughter!" What was startling in that moment was the panic on the student's face, her realization that she had contributed to this moment. I could just hear the voices in her head: 'Mom, I didn't do the homework.' But unfortunately Mom had already committed to the story and neither the student nor I could challenge her without making the situation worse.

A few months later, the student finally confided in me that she had not done the assignment because she had been way too busy practicing for her upcoming dance audition for the school musical. She expressed how embarrassed and sorry she was about the incident. She had learnt a lesson about integrity.

In another case, students were to write an original poem for homework. When I read this student's poem it was clear to me that the language was way above what I was accustomed to in previous writing samples. When I asked her if she had written the poem she said yes. I checked to see if the poem was her original work but it was not – she had lifted straight from the Internet.

Needless to say, she earned herself a zero and I notified her father about the failing grade. Dad was irate when he came to parent night. He said he had stayed up all night with her and they'd worked on it together. He never left her side. When I showed him that the poem appeared elsewhere on the Web, he was shocked and embarrassed. It wasn't my intention to make an enemy of Dad. There again, was a parent who was willing to compromise his position as a guide. In my opinion, this is a misguided form of love.

One of our biggest jobs as parents is to demonstrate the subtleties of integrity in all areas of life. It is not always an easy task. Reframing makes things easier. In his book on integrity, Clinical Psychologist Dr. Henry Cloud defines character as "the ability to meet the demands of reality." The reality is – students must do quality homework, research and prepare themselves to participate in the classroom discourse in order to become leaders on the world stage. Furthermore, it is the culture of college, career and private life to prepare and practice. That lawyer, neurologist, corrections officer, teacher, chef, novelist or that florist in your child must make time to do quality homework – it is a reality of life.

If we live with integrity, we give our children the opportunity to choose this value as they grow. However it's never too late to cultivate integrity. The student in our first story got an opportunity to immediately see and feel the effects of her decision in play. It could have been worse. She could have let Mom's story remain unchallenged. She could have refused to acknowledge her own error in judgement. Sometimes our zeal to make our children perfect is a reflection of our own need to appear perfect. That little child inside the parent, the one who fabricated stories to avoid punishment is still trying to be perfect. Perfection is impossible. Let's reach for integrity.

Affirmation: *As a parent, I leave competition and pretending behind. I know myself, I know my children. I understand that a strong character is necessary for my children to lead a successful life. From my stillness, I know how to teach them this universal principle.*

Chapter 32

Effort

By failing to prepare you are preparing to fail.

−Ben Franklin

How would your kids like it if dinner meat came out of the kitchen practically raw or laundry day was a series of shortcuts or didn't happen at all? Undercooked food would be causing them foodborne illnesses and their days at school would be a parade of smelly clothes and horrified friends. As parents and teachers, we have to go to great lengths and ask students the same questions when they take shortcuts and don't produce their best work.

My high school juniors and I had spent quality time, four days to be exact, analyzing Langston Hughes' essay, *The Artist and the Racial Mountain*. We addressed language, metaphors, the arguments, style, themes, social and historical context and relevance.

Friday morning, it was time to test them on six critical thinking questions to see what they had learned. When I sat down to grade the papers, I realized that 80% of the class had paraphrased the questions, regurgitated key points in the prompt, passing them off as fully-developed responses. They had used one of the oldest tricks in the book.

How could this happen in a class of 16 year-old students? Whether we like it or not, the hated exams – SAT, AP – were coming up in 120 days. Even if you are not a proponent of testing, these rules of writing should not be crammed only to be forgotten. They are prerequisites for college and lifetime of communication. According to HigherEducation.Org, "60% of freshmen have to pay for non-credit remedial English."

It's a waste to pay for non-credit remedial English when precious finances should be directed to other needs including study-abroad programs. The solution: master English in high school. By the end of their Junior year, students should have mastered the argument, narrative, expository, synthesis essays and written a winning personal statement for college. These were smart kids. Yet they were in danger of becoming part of the epidemic of ill-prepared students desperately seeking help to write their college essay. They would be ruling out attendance to top colleges and winning big scholarships. I tried to get to the bottom of the matter. Somebody had not called them on this type of behavior. I listened attentively as they recited their litany of woes, how they are painfully trying to balance school with extracurricular activities. I would have none of it.

    I devised a way to teach them the content and gave them time management skills. We went into high gear and spent another week collaborating, line by line, idea by idea so they could internalize the principles. They practiced listening in order to ask high level questions that advanced the discussions. They learned to listen deeply and respect each other's position on topics that emerged during the discourse. Then I went down my list of time management tips and stress busters. I reminded them about focusing and getting into the zone. There are always going to be distractions and we may not always find a quiet space to work.

    We have to break the cycle when children give a song-and-dance about an assignment. Both teacher and parent should do due diligence. Call them on it every time. They are never too grown for parents to check their schoolwork. In my role, I extend an invitation to the student to help them work on challenging material and difficult concepts. Parents can do that too. Some parents will say they don't understand Trigonometry or Mandarin. It doesn't matter. The first thing is to identify that the student has a failing grade. Often, students will leave their papers that earned an "F" grade behind in the classroom because they don't want to be reprimanded by their parents. Put a preventive measure in place. Talk to the teacher regularly.

Researchers at Brigham Young, North Carolina State and University of California confirmed the power of the parent in a national study with more than 10,000 students, along with their parents, teachers and school administrators. Their goal was to determine the role of school social capital and family social capital. They found that while both were important, "the role of family involvement is stronger when it comes to academic success." They defined parent involvement as checking homework, attending school meetings and events and discussing school activities at home.

At home, help us to help the student. Reinforce those time management skills and stress busters I mentioned earlier. Help your children generate better schedules and help them take breaks. In her research, former NASA scientist Joan Vernikos found that sitting for extended periods of time instead of moving against gravity can cause the body stress and in the case of people in the mid-30s, premature aging. If you have young gamers at home and they are sitting for long periods of time, monitor their video gaming. Get them to move around every 20-30 minutes. What about the best time to work? A surprising number of people have found themselves able to do their best work in the early morning. Students were no different. Leaving study until late night does not always produce optimum results. Study earlier and nap before studying. Geniuses Leonardo da Vinci and Nikola Tesla napped a lot to get their creative juices going.

    Pay keen attention so you can recognize the song-and-dance you get from your children. Too many are graduating from high schools and colleges, barely literate. Some become a danger to themselves. Others are devastated because they are embarrassed, their dignity crushed. Some may not be as lucky as Dexter Manley, pro-bowl defensive end for the Redskins who got a high paying job despite the fact he couldn't read. Fortunately he built up enough courage to ask for help and learned to read and write in his later years. Learn from other examples. Our young students don't have to have that experience to succeed.

Affirmation: *In this moment, I am doing my best work. I am doing everything I can do to get the very best results. I encourage my children to do the same and demonstrate this ability for them.*

Chapter 33

Adaptability

It is not the strongest of the species that survives, nor the most intelligent that survives. It is the one that is most adaptable to change.

−Charles Darwin

Change is the most constant part of nature, yet, it can be the most unwelcome, unfriendly, even hostile part of our human existence. Sometimes we find ourselves at the center of dramatic shifts that bring our raw emotions to the surface and make us feel vulnerable. Life throws us curveballs. How the adaptable among us respond to crises can be inspirational.

When starfish lose their limbs in underwater battles, they go through a period of regeneration and they regrow the limbs. Veteran and double amputee Senator Tammy Duckworth got new limbs after her helicopter was shot down over Iraq in 2004, but these limbs are nothing like those of the starfish. In a 2012 interview with *Mother Jones Magazine,* we found out that it wasn't easy for the former Blackhawk pilot to get around wearing those prosthetics and run for Congress. One limb is joined at the hip. It doesn't make for comfortable meet and greets on the campaign trail but she gets the job done without complaints.

Duckworth is unusual. Before her injury, she was a woman determined to adapt and serve in military combat, still considered to be a man's world. She lost her two legs and nearly lost her arm in the bargain and still continued to serve in the military. Now she's the first disabled woman veteran to serve in the Senate and her role is no less demanding. She doesn't consider her circumstances unusual. She takes it all in stride. She continues to battle for military vets and for the citizens of Illinois. For her, fatigue, chronic imbalance and phantom pain are not deterrents. Adaptability is adjusting to the reality of her new body and moving forward.

Adaptability also demands a full retreat to see the big picture in order to gain new ground. I am forever fascinated with the biology of the elongated giant squid. The squid is highly adaptable. It's flexible, agile, nimble and open to change. At times, it spews ink-like substance into the water to retreat from danger and protect itself from predators.

One fall semester, I found myself looking to the squid for inspiration. I returned to school and to the new reality of no permanent classroom for my 200 plus ever expanding roster of scholars. I was given a portable food cart to house my library, supplies, student work and personal belongings. The height of the cart was below my waistline and was a terrible strain on my near six feet tall frame. The weight and the wheels made it difficult to push the cart through the hallways and over door thresholds. Books and papers for my five courses kept falling off at every turn. I felt abused, punished, dishonored and neglected. Privately I cried.

The more I focused on those feelings, the greater the physical pain. Then I had to learn a new way of commuting in the building. When it was time for a quick bathroom break, I negotiated with students to watch my belongings. Then one day, I realized there were still 170 more days of the school year to go. It was time to change the way I responded to the situation or I would literally expire. Like the squid, I retreated from danger, in this case, my own anger. And when I did, I found joy in my classroom experience which took the sting out of my travails with the cart.

Whether it's a divorce, a new blended family, changing school, a new address, children are constantly being tested as well. They may respond to these changes with higher stress levels. We can model adaptability for our children. Talking with them about the event, even more than once before it occurs, helps to prepare the child for the change and lowers the stress. Mealtime and bedtime are opportunities for adaptability training. Staying on a schedule with both those activities creates attitudes about change.

Sending the child off to school on the first day is a test. But we do our best to transition through it: putting out clothes the night before, packing lunch, walking to the school bus; waving goodbye and an encouraging voice has gone a long way. We have seen it for centuries. The qualities that our children build from these traumatic incidents are the same qualities that lead them through difficult changes later in life and work.

As parents, we are here to reflect light for our children – to be bioluminescent as the squid in the dark ocean. As Major Tammy Duckworth watched the *Trinity Irish Dancers* perform at an outdoor concert back in

2012, curious children came up to examine her prosthetics, one of which happens to be camouflage. One of the mother's in the crowd, possibly transferring her own feelings of discomfort or good manners, said to her child, "Don't stare."

However, I say this would be the time to let the children become captivated by Tammy Duckworth's adaptability story. It will come in handy when self-encouragement is necessary. What was I to learn from my cart story? I was pushing the cart to bring light into my classroom for thirty plus children waiting to unleash their own light onto the world. I'm pushing the cart to gain upper-body strength for my physical journey through life. The very nature of the universe is change and we have to adapt to those changes.

Affirmation: *In this moment, I accept that my present situation is teaching me to be open to the change I need to advance and grow. I help my child do the same. My children see my good attitude towards my life experience and adapt those good qualities into shaping the direction of their lives.*

References

Introduction

Angelou, Maya. (1969) *I Know Why The Caged Bird Sings*. New York, NY: Random House

Does Capital at home matter more than capital at School? Social capital effects on academic achievement. Mikaela Dufur, Toby L. Parcell and Kelly P. Troutman. Science Direct Volume 31, March 2013, pp 1-21.

Chapter 1

Academy of Achievement (Producer). (1991, February 21). The Queen of Daytime TV. Oprah Winfrey Academy of Achievement Interview. Chicago IL. Retrieved from: http://www.achievement.org/achiever/oprah-winfrey/#interview

Werner, Emmy. (2005). Resilience and Recovery: Findings From The Kauai Longitudinal Study. FOCAL POINT: Research, Policy and Practice in Children's Mental Health. 19 (1), 11-14 Retrieved from https://www.pathwaysrtc.pdx.edu/pdf/fpS0504.pdf

Chapter 2

Wing, Lorna (1981). Asperger syndrome: a clinical account. MRC Social Psychiatry Unit, Institute of Psychiatry, London. Retrieved from: http://www.mugsy.org/wing2.htm

Chapter 3

Robinson, Kenneth. (2006, February). Do Schools Kill Creativity? TED. Lecture. Retrieved from: ttps://www.ted.com/talks/ken_robinson_says_schools_kill_creativity

Chapter 4

Housing Families First. (2017, April 28). Life at a homeless shelter when you are 6. Retrieved from: http://www.housingfamiliesfirst.org/2017/04/28/life-at-a-homeless-shelter-when-youre-6.

Sellers, Patricia. (2015, April 28). A former Accenture exec, once homeless, leads the National Guard's efforts to quell the Baltimore Riots. Fortune Magazine. [Originally published August 19, 2013] Retrieved from: http://www.fortune.com/2015/04/28/accenture-exec-once-homeless-is-a-general/

Chapter 5

Lopez, Steve. (2015, May 27). Willpower, Wisdom fuel 99-year-old's quest for a college degree. Los Angeles Times. Retrieved from: www.latimes.com/local/california/la-me-0527-lopez-doreetha-2-20150519-column.html

Chapter 6

Castro, C.A.; Hoge, C.W.; Cox, A.L. (2006) Battlemind Training: Building Soldier Resiliency. In Human Dimensions in Military Operations – Military Leaders' Strategies for Addressing Stress and Psychological Support (pp. 42-1 – 42-6). Meeting Proceedings RTO-MP-HFM-134, Paper 42. Neuilly-sur-Seine, France: RTO. Retrieved from: http://www.rto.nato.int/abstracts.asp.

Chapter 7

Murray, Rebecca. (2016, February 17). Will Smith Talks About "The Pursuit of Happyness" ThoughtCo.Com. Retrieved from: https://www.thoughtco.com/will-smith-talks-pursuit-of-happyness-2431458

Chapter 8

Blue Light Has A Dark Side: Expose to blue light at night, emitted by electronics and energy-efficient lightbulbs, harmful to your healthy. (2015, September 2). Harvard Health Letter. Harvard Health Publications. Retrieved from: https://www.health.harvard.edu/staying-healthy/blue-light-has-a-dark-side: First published May 2012

Chapter 9

Hart, Betty., Risley, Todd R. (2003, Spring). The Early Catastrophe. The 30 Million Word Gap. American Education v27 n1 p4-9 Retrieved from: file:///C:/Users/Faith/Downloads/Hart%20Ridley%20Stud7y%201995.pdf

Chapter 10

Farber, Sharon K. (2006, August 10) The Inner Predator: Trauma and Dissociation in Bodily Self Harm. New Orleans APA Panel "Trauma: Obvious and Hidden: Possibilities for Treatment August 10, 2006. Retrieved from http://www.apadivisions.org/division-39/sections/childhood/farber.pdf?_ga=2.141745074.1615721198.1502459831-451534378.1498601940

Slepian, Michael L., Chun, J.S., & Mason, M. F. (2017) The Experience of Secrecy. Journal of Personality and

Social Psychology. Retrieved from: http://www.columbia.edu/~ms4992/Research.htm

Slepian, Michael L., Masicampo, E. J., and Ambady, Nalini. (2014) Relieving the Burdens of Secrecy: Revealing Secrets Influences Judgments of Hill Slant and Distance. Social Psychological and Personality Science. 5(3) 293-300 Retrieved from http://www.columbia.edu/~ms4992/Pubs/2014_Slepian-MasicampAmbady_RevealingSecrets_SPPS.pdf

Chapter 11

The American Academy of Child and Adolescent Psychiatry. (2011) Children and Divorce. Facts for Families Vol 01. Retrieved from http://www.aascap.org

Chapter 12

Simmons, Rachel (Feb 2017) Failing Well: Campus Series Helps Students Rethink Setbacks – Smith College Grecourt Gate. Retrieved from: http://www.smith.edu/news

Chapter 13

Violence and Homicide Among Youth. Gateway to Health Communication & Social Marketing Practice. Centers for Disease Control and Prevention. June 24, 2015.

https://www.cdc.gov.healthcommunication/toolstem plates/entertainmented/tips/violenceyouth.html (Accessed August 16, 2017)

Kubler-Ross, Elisabeth, and Kessler, David. (2005) On Grief and Grieving: Finding the Meaning of Grief Through the Five Stages of Loss. New York, NY: Scribner.

Chapter 14

American Psychological Association (n.d.) Communication tips for parents. Psychology Help Center. Retrieved from: http://www.apa.org/helpcenter

Keirsey, David. (1998) Please Understand Me II: Temperament, Character Intelligence. Delmar CA: Prometheus Nemesis Book Company. Chapter 8

Chapter 15

Brown, Brené. (Nov 2012) The Relationship Between Joy and Gratitude. Well Being Series: Taking Charge of Your Health. Center for Spirituality and Healing. University of Minnesota. Retrieved from https://www.takingcharge.csh.umn.edu/ daring-be-vulnerable-brene-brown.

Chapter 16

Stryker, Rod. (2011) The Four Desires: Creating a Life of Purpose, Happiness, Prosperity and Freedom. New York, NY: Delacorte Press, Pg 186.

Murphy Paul, Annie. (2013) The Science of Smart: How the Power of Intention Can Help You Learn Better. NOVA – Secret Life of Scientists Blog. Retrieved from http://www.pbs.org/wgbh/nova/blogs/secretlife/blog posts/the-smart-of-science-how-the-power-of-intention-can-help-you-learn-better/

Chapter 17

Ruiz, Don Miguel. (1997) The Four Agreements: A Practical Guide To Personal Freedom. San Rafael, CA: Amber-Allen Publishing

Chapter 18

Jones Ph.D., Jo., Mosher Ph.D., William D. (2013, December 20) Fathers' Involvement With Their Children: United States 2006-2010. Division of Vital Statistics. No. 71. Retrieved from http://www.cdc.gov

Chapter 19

Epston, David. (1999) Co-research: The making of an alternative knowledge. Narrative Therapy and Community Work: A Conference Collection ...

Adelaide, AU: Dulwich Centre Publications. Retrieved from Dulwitchcentre.com.au.

Chapter 20

Public Radio International: The World (2015, March 12) Memory Banda escaped child marriage in Malawi, but her 11-year-old sister wasn't so lucky. Joyce Hackel, Producer. Across Women's Lives – Body Politics: The struggle for reproductive rights. Retrieved from http://www.pri.org

Chapter 21

https://studentaid.ed.gov/sa/sites/default/files/college-prep-checklist.pdf

Chapter 22

Grazer, Brian., and Fishman, Charles. (2015) A Curious Mind? The Secret to a Bigger Life. New York, NY: Simon & Schuster

Chapter 23

OWN Network (Producer). (2013, July 7). Redefining The Role Of A Father. Oprah's Life Class. Retrieved from https://www.youtube.com/watch?v=dgrcdE6E9O8

US Department of Health and Human Services. Child Welfare Information Gateway. (2006). *The Importance of*

Fathers in the Healthy Development of Children. Child Abuse and Neglect User Manual Series. Retrieved from https://www.childwelfare.gov/pubs/usermanuals/fatherhood

Cohn, D'Vera., Caumant, Andrea. (2014, April 8) 7 Key Findings About Stay At Home Moms. Fact Tank: News In The Numbers. Retrieved from http://www.pewresearch.org

Latvala, Charlotte. (2011) The New Stay-At-Home Mom. Parenting Magazine Blog. Retrieved from http://www.parenting.com/article/the-new-stay-at-home-mom

Hager, Dean, J. (2016, April 26) The Real Reason Behind The Tech Skills Gap. Fortune Magazine. Fortune Insiders. Retrieved from http://fortune.com/2016/04/27/tech-skills-gap-stem/

Chapter 24

Rosenthal, Dr., Norman. (n.d.) How Meditation Changed Hugh Jackman's Life. Oprah.com Retrieved from: http://www.oprah.com/inspiration/how-meditation-changed-hugh-jackmans-life

Chapter 25

Vale, Ronald D. (2013, March 15). The value of asking questions. Molecular Biology of the Cell.24(6); 680-682. Retrieved from: https://www.ncbi.nlm.nih.gov/pmc/articles/PMC3596240/

Chapter 26

Gopnik, Ph.D., Alison. (2009, April 4). The Philosophical Baby: What Children's Minds Tell Us About Truth, Love, and the Meaning of Life. New York, NY: Farrar, Straus and Giroux.

Chapter 27

Gross, Rebecca. (2014, November 14). Fighting Illiteracy, One Poem At A Time. National Endowment For The Arts. Arts Works Blog. Retrieved from: https://www.arts.gov/art-works/2014/fighting-illiteracy-one-poem-at-a-time

Meisinger, Elizabeth B., Schwanenflugel, Paula J., Bradley, Barbara A., & Stahl, Steven A. (2004, June 1). Interaction Quality during Partner Reading. Journal of Literary Research. 36(2), 111-140. Retrieved from: https://www.ncbi.nlm.nih.gov/pmc/articles/PMC2760827/

Chapter 28

Bennett, Abbie. (2017, July 9). Priest in a red corvette pulls out a gun in a road-rage incident police say. Miami Herald. Retrieved from: http://www.miamiherald.com/news/nation-world/national/article160389659.html

King, Peter H. (2001, May 27). A Moment of Road Rage Changes Lives Forever. Los Angeles Times. Retrieved from: http://articles.latimes.com/2001/may/27/local/me-3290

Chapter 29

Marley, Bob. (1970). Corner Stone. [Recorded by Bob Marley and the Wailers]. On Soul Rebel [Album]. Kingston, Jamaica: Maroon.

Steel, Charles., Bing, Steve., Blackwell, Chris., & Marley, Ziggy (Producers), & McDonald, Kevin (Director). (2012). Marley (Documentary Film). United Kingdom: Universal Pictures

Chapter 30

Tortello, Dr., Rebecca. (n.d.). Captivated by Jamaica. Pieces of the Past Series. Jamaica Gleaner. Retrieved from: http://old.jamaica-gleaner.com/pages/history/story0033.html

Aronson, Steven M. L., (2000, March 31). Jamaica's Golden Eye: The Birthplace of James Bond is Recast as a Luxury Resort. Architectural Digest Magazine. Culture and Lifestyle Section. Retrieved from: https://www.architecturaldigest.com/story/hotels-goldeneye-042000

Chapter 31

Cloud, Henry. (2006). Integrity: The courage to meet the demands of reality: How six essential qualities determine your success in business. New York, NY: Harper Collins

Chapter 32

Vernikos, Ph.D., Joan. (2011, December). Sitting Kills, Moving Heals: How Simple Everyday Movement Will Prevent Pain, Illness, and Early Death – And Exercises Alone Won't. Fresno, CA: Quill Driver Books

Chapter 33

Weinstein, Adam. (2012, August). Nobody Puts Tammy Duckworth in a Corner. Mother Jones Politics. Retrieved from: http://www.motherjones.com/politics/2012/08/tammy-duckworth-versus-joe-walsh-congress/

Acknowledgements

It all started with the question: How can you help me to help my children? The quintessential inquiry came from the real heroes that inspired this book: the many parents with whom I interact at educational seminars, parent-teacher conferences, commuting on the New York City subways, Metro North, in the supermarket parking lots, synagogues, churches and pharmacies. Parents who want me to help them figure out how to help their children succeed in school, college and career.

High praise belongs to Faith Nelson of *Story Depot* who brought her research, development, design and coaching skills to every step of the way with this project.

Thanks to Olympian, International Motivational Keynote Speaker, author, philanthropist, Devon Harris for giving us permission to write a story about him in, *Stories to Heal Your Life*. Again, Faith said, "A story about Devon Harris belongs in this book." Here it is.

To those who entrusted me with your compelling stories, thanks for sharing. For those of you who preferred anonymity, I applaud your boldness and will continue to honor your privacy.

The series title, *From A Teacher to Parents* grew out of a writing workshop, *Pitch Perfect & Blurbalicious: How to Present Your Project with Maximum Agent-Editor-Reader Appeal* facilitated by multi-title romance suspense author,

Alice Orr at *The International Women's Writing Guild's* 2015 Spring Big Apple Conference in New York City.

Beta-Reading services were provided by Sandra Bonner-James, educator and social services professional (retired). She offered valuable insight and encouragement to keep telling these stories. Heartfelt thanks to Keisha Lloyd of *Rivage Speakers Bureau* for representation.

The team at *Sisal Publishing* has been exceptionally gracious and has gone over and above to make this book a reality in 2017, for this, I am grateful.

Then there is family. Thanks to all for cheering me on and giving me much needed support to balance family life, teaching and writing.

From A Teacher To Parents: Stories to Heal Your Life So You Can Help Your Child Succeed is a love offering to families from a tender place in my heart to yours.

Literacy Gateway Institute

Literacy Gateway Institute, Inc., is an educational solution business focused on success, innovation and access for all learners. The Institute develops and implements learning systems and curricula, improves student performance in content area and standardized tests, and facilitates results-driven interaction between educational institutions and the communities they serve.

literacygatewayinstitute.com

www.ingramcontent.com/pod-product-compliance
Lightning Source LLC
Chambersburg PA
CBHW030435010526
44118CB00011B/642